W9-BQI-593

Maids

Katie Skelly

To My Sister

FANTAGRAPHICS BOOKS INC. — 7563 Lake City Way NE — Seattle, Washington 98115 — www.fantagraphics.com

EDITOR AND ASSOCIATE PUBLISHER:
 Eric Reynolds
BOOK DESIGN: Jacob Covey
PRODUCTION: Paul Baresh
PUBLISHER: Gary Groth

ISBN 978-1-68396-368-4
LIBRARY OF CONGRESS CONTROL NUMBER
2020935010

SECOND PRINTING: February 2021
Printed in China

CHAPTER

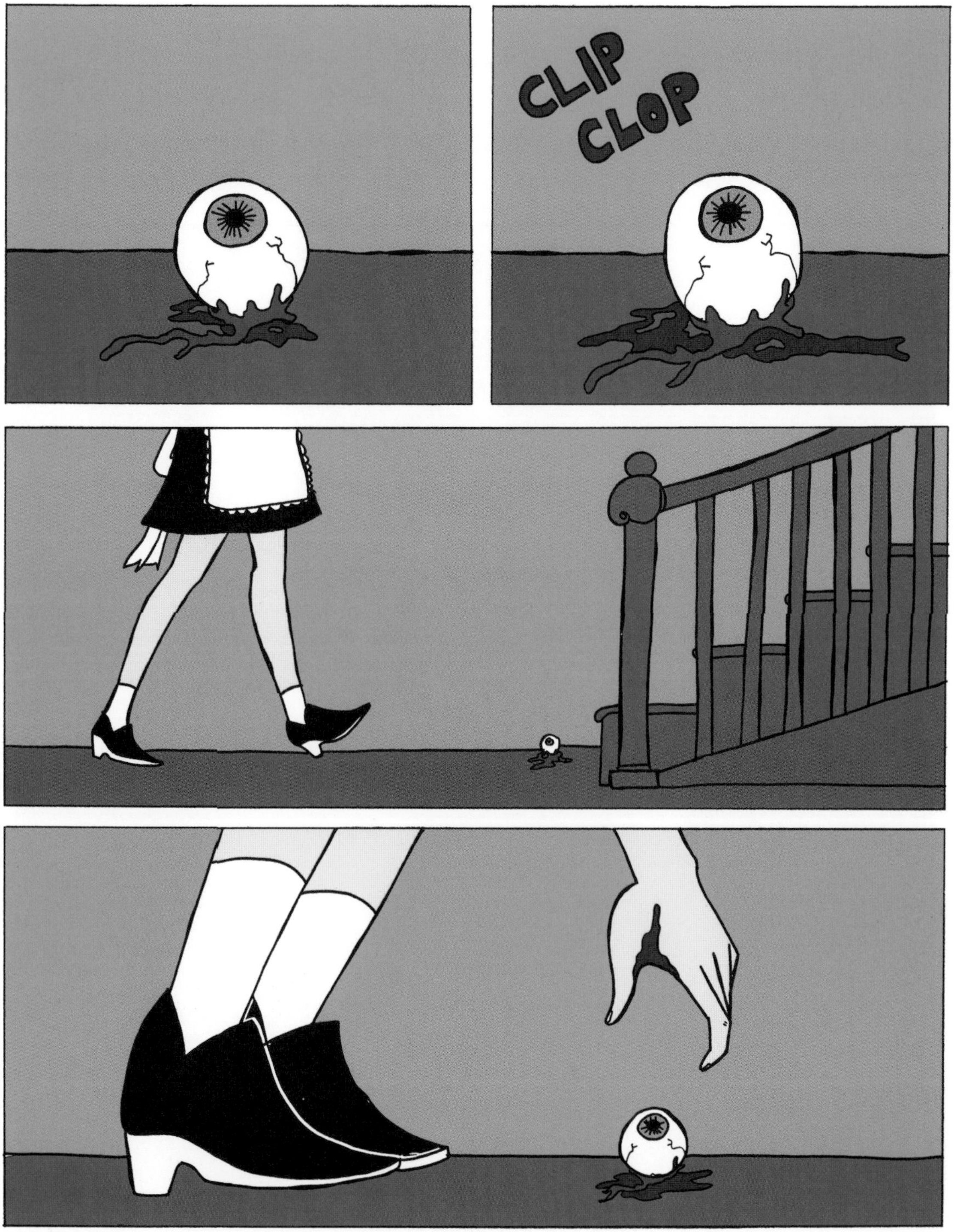
CLIP
CLOP

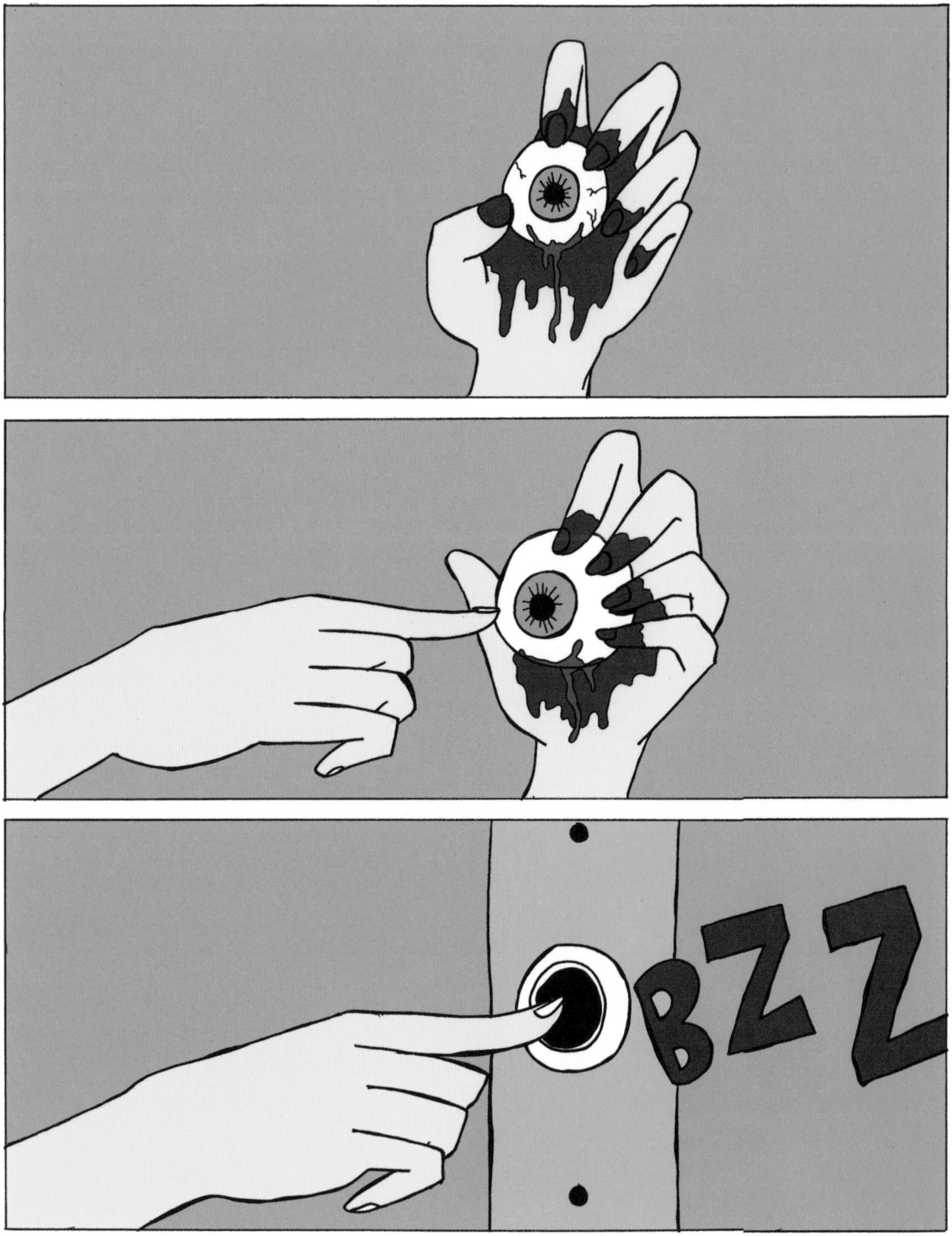
BZZ

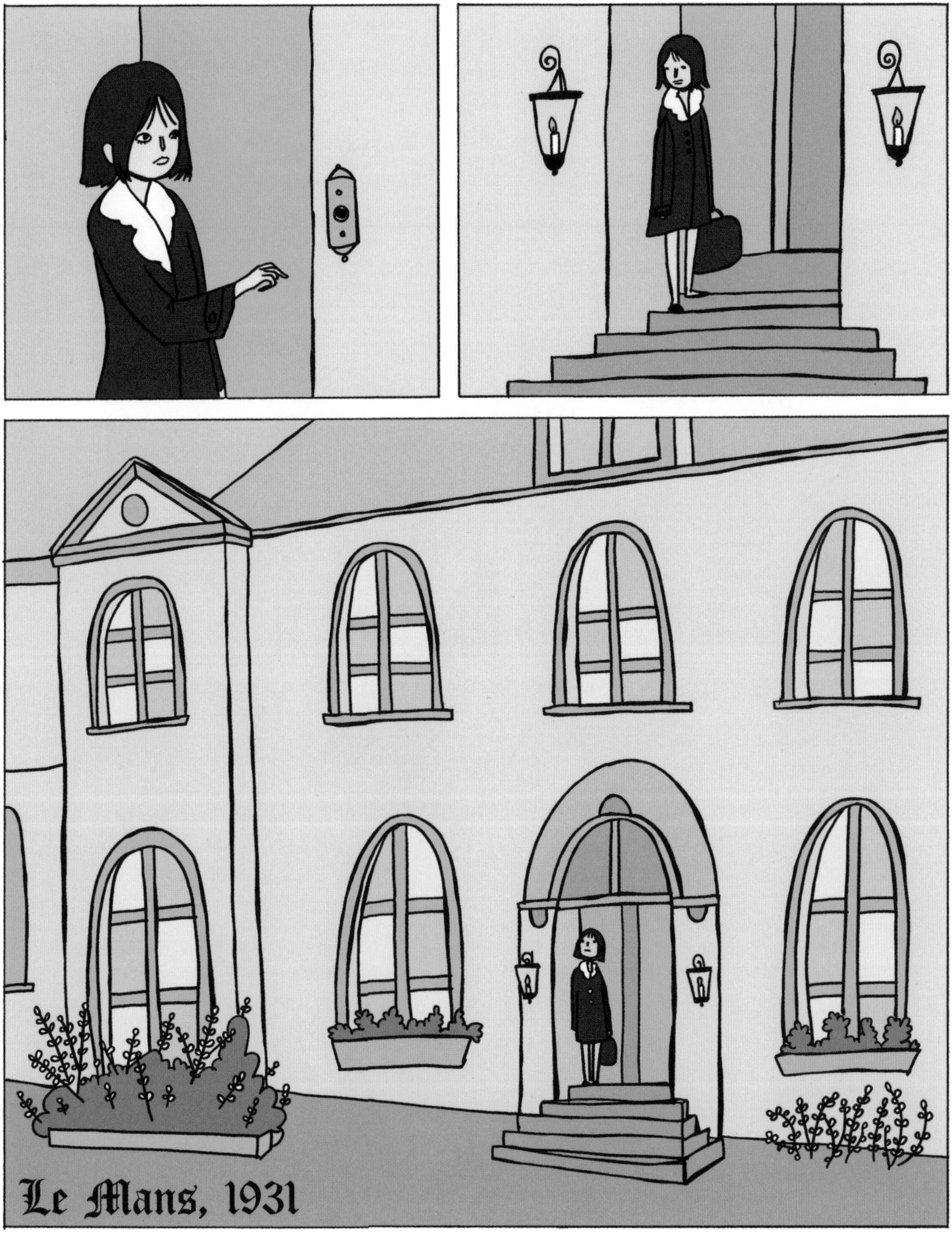
Le Mans, 1931

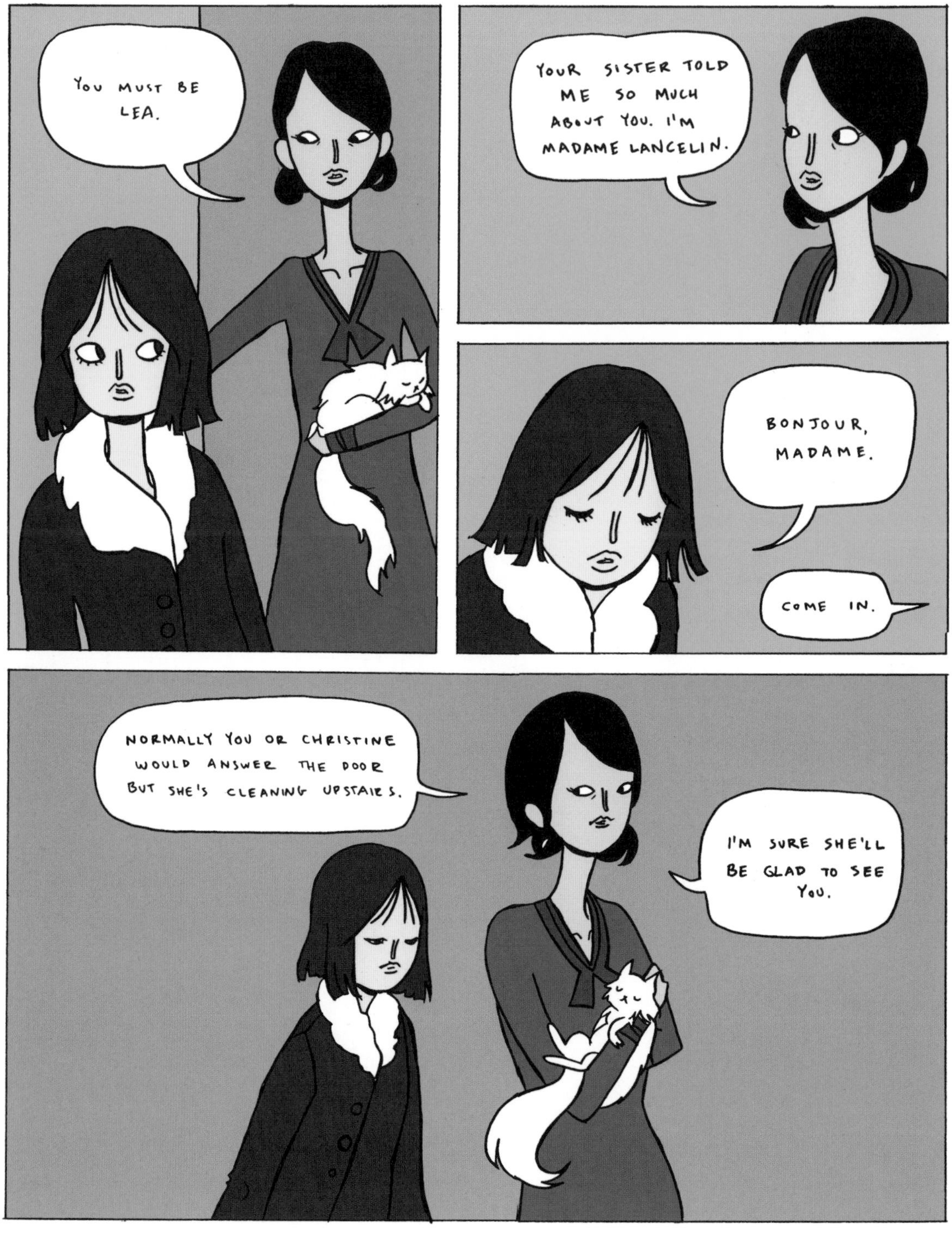
YOU MUST BE LEA.
YOUR SISTER TOLD ME SO MUCH ABOUT YOU. I'M MADAME LANCELIN.
BONJOUR, MADAME.
COME IN.
NORMALLY YOU OR CHRISTINE WOULD ANSWER THE DOOR BUT SHE'S CLEANING UPSTAIRS.
I'M SURE SHE'LL BE GLAD TO SEE YOU.

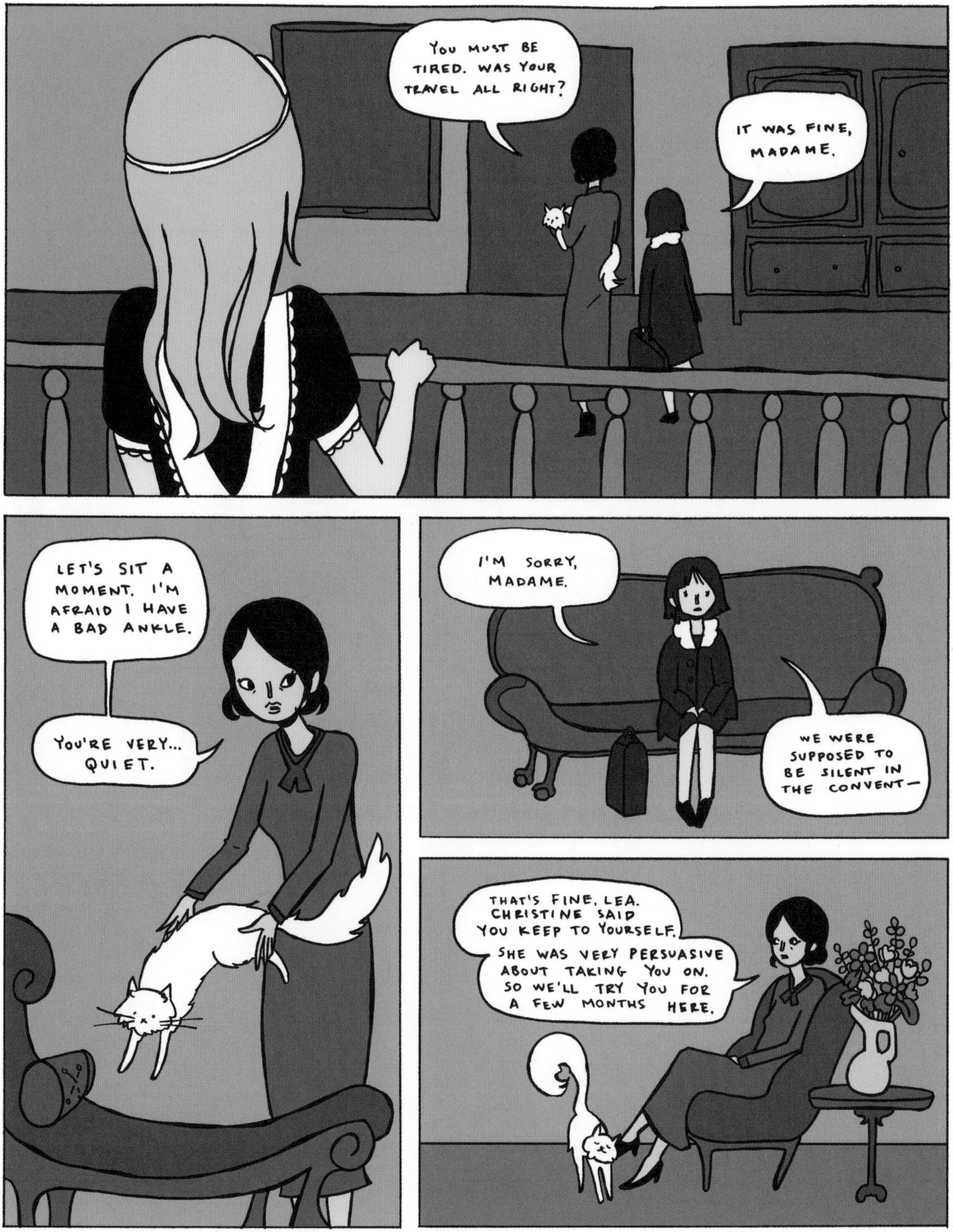
YOU MUST BE TIRED. WAS YOUR TRAVEL ALL RIGHT?
IT WAS FINE, MADAME.
LET'S SIT A MOMENT. I'M AFRAID I HAVE A BAD ANKLE.
YOU'RE VERY... QUIET.
I'M SORRY, MADAME.
WE WERE SUPPOSED TO BE SILENT IN THE CONVENT—
THAT'S FINE, LEA. CHRISTINE SAID YOU KEEP TO YOURSELF.
SHE WAS VERY PERSUASIVE ABOUT TAKING YOU ON. SO WE'LL TRY YOU FOR A FEW MONTHS HERE.

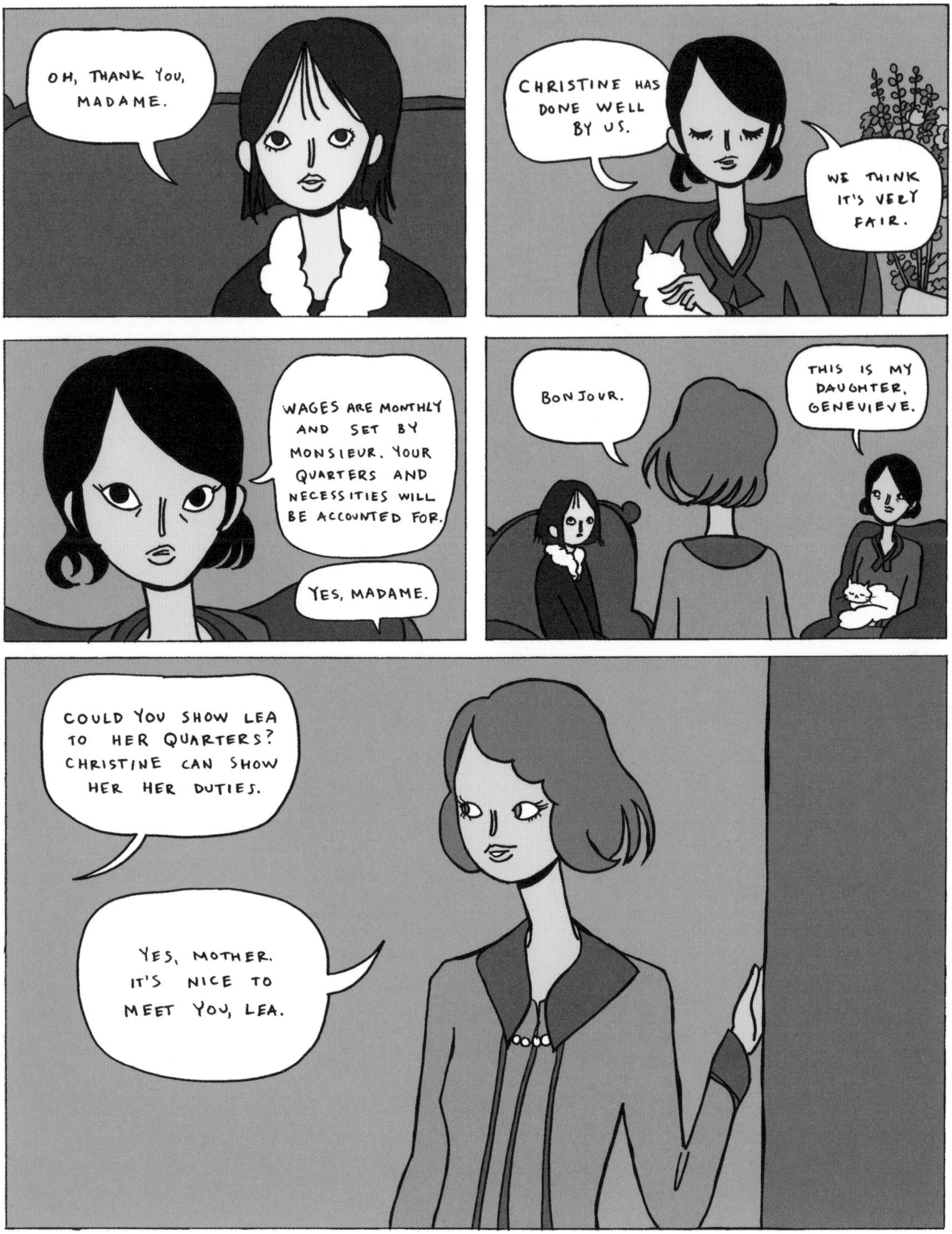
OH, THANK YOU, MADAME.
CHRISTINE HAS DONE WELL BY US.
WE THINK IT'S VERY FAIR.
WAGES ARE MONTHLY AND SET BY MONSIEUR. YOUR QUARTERS AND NECESSITIES WILL BE ACCOUNTED FOR.
YES, MADAME.
BONJOUR.
THIS IS MY DAUGHTER, GENEVIEVE.
COULD YOU SHOW LEA TO HER QUARTERS? CHRISTINE CAN SHOW HER HER DUTIES.
YES, MOTHER. IT'S NICE TO MEET YOU, LEA.

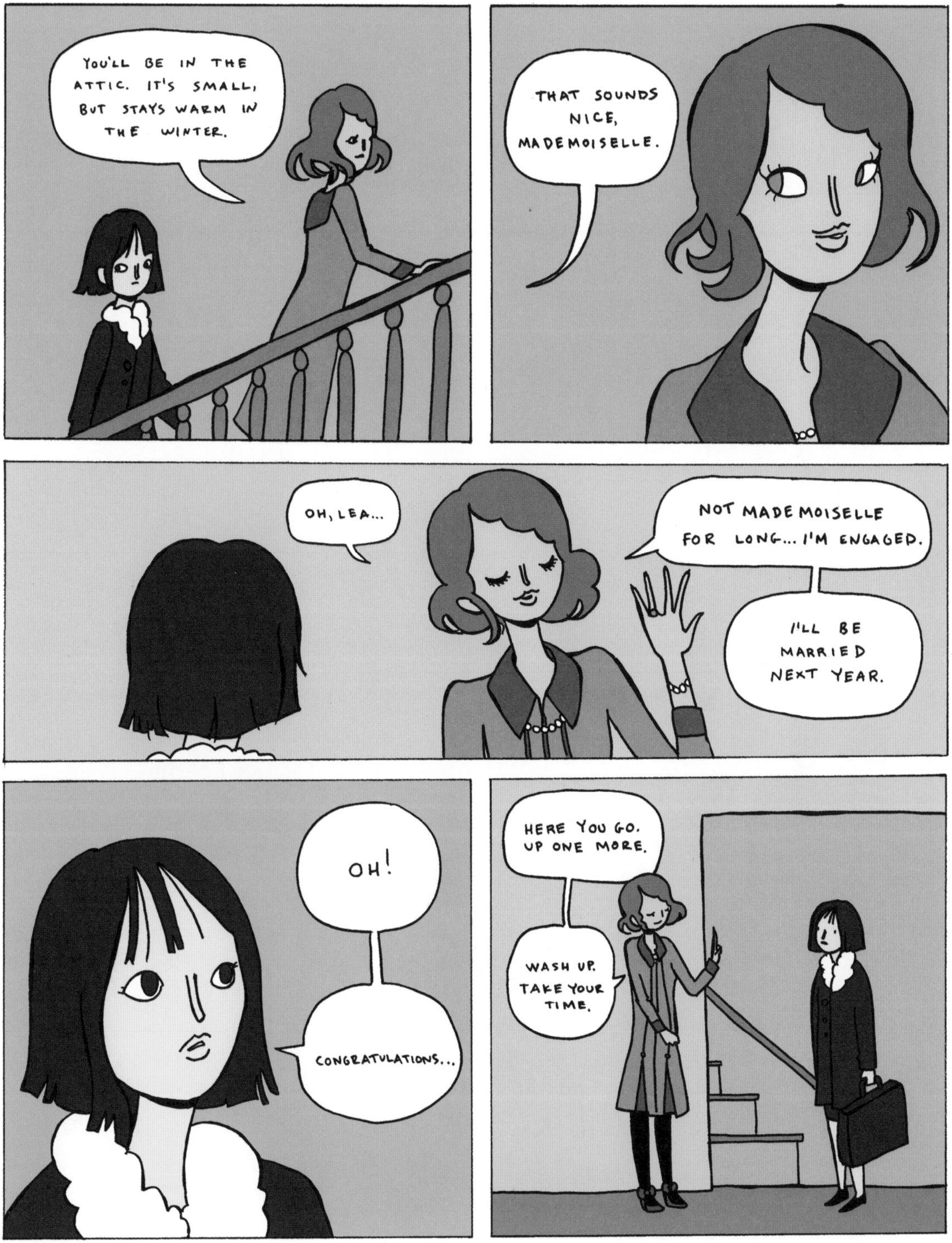
YOU'LL BE IN THE ATTIC. IT'S SMALL, BUT STAYS WARM IN THE WINTER.
THAT SOUNDS NICE, MADEMOISELLE.
OH, LEA...
NOT MADEMOISELLE FOR LONG... I'M ENGAGED.
I'LL BE MARRIED NEXT YEAR.
OH!
CONGRATULATIONS...
HERE YOU GO. UP ONE MORE.
WASH UP. TAKE YOUR TIME.

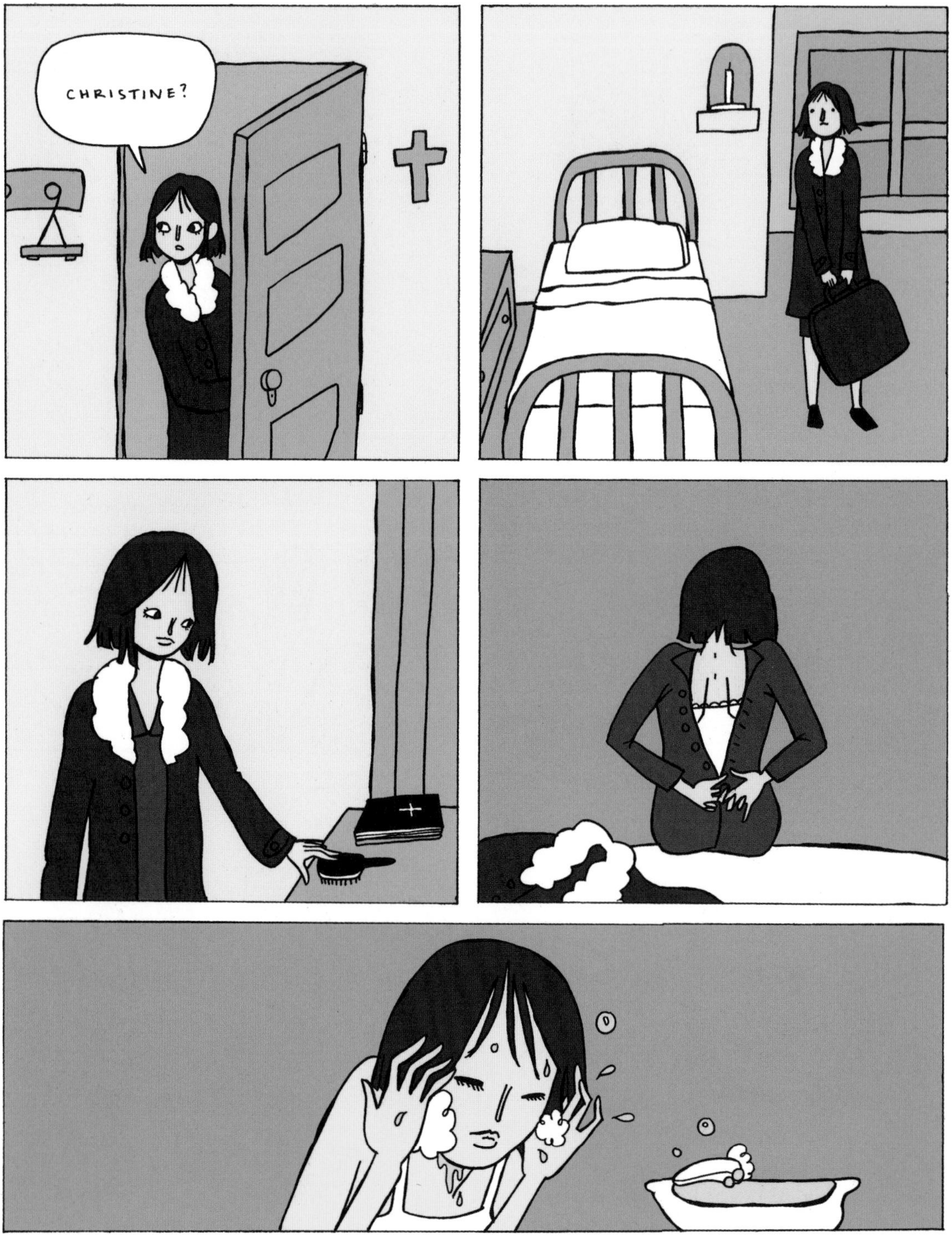
CHRISTINE?

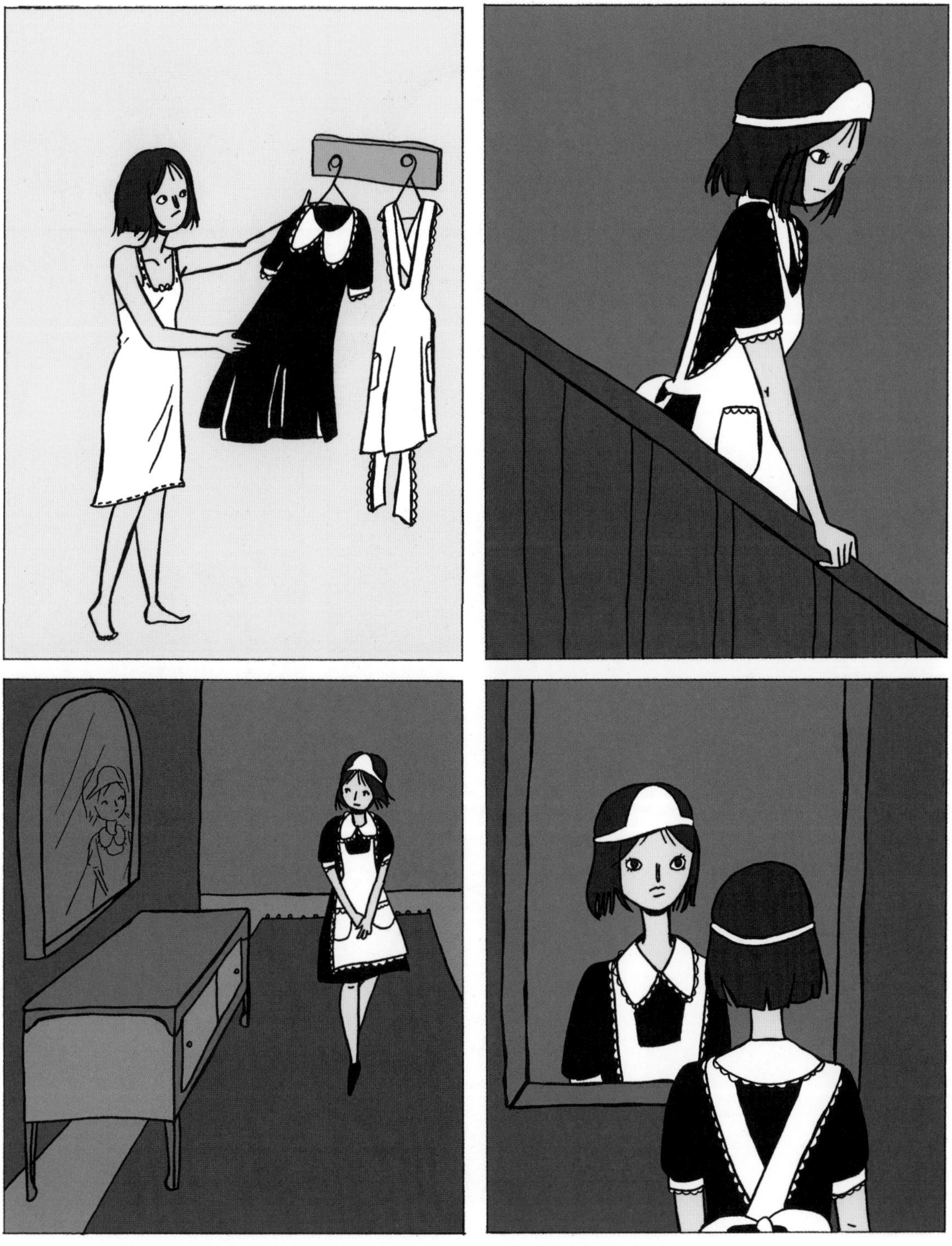

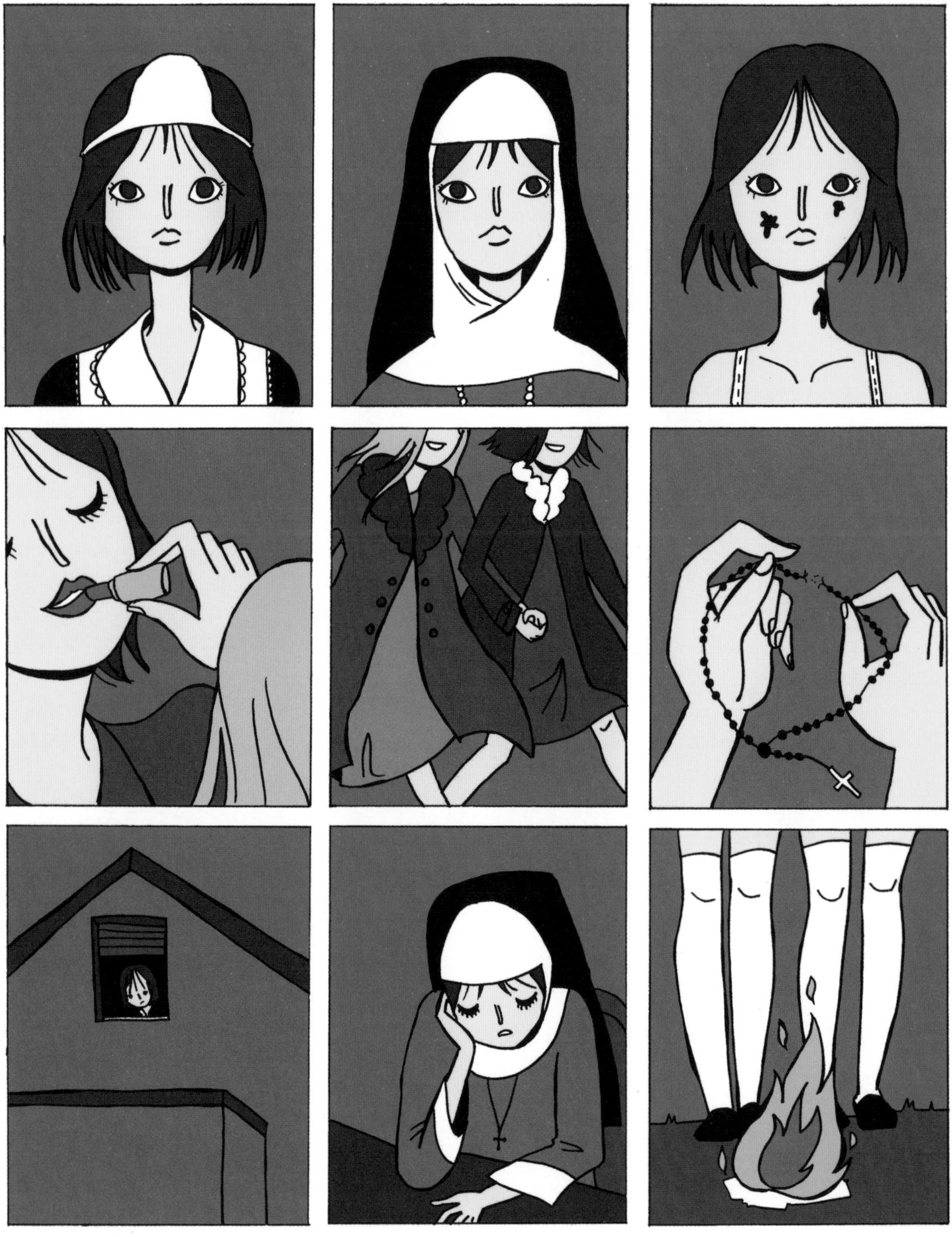

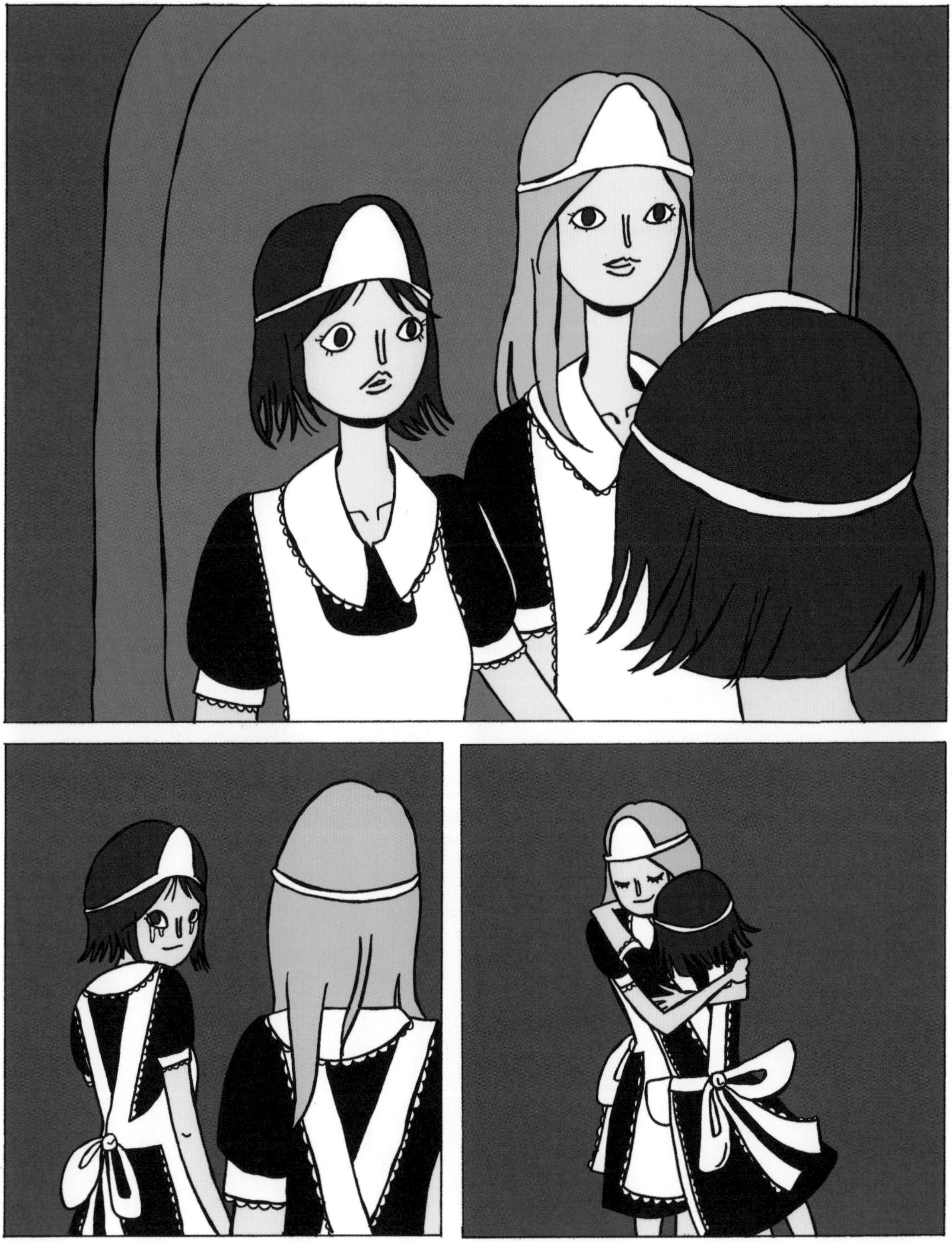

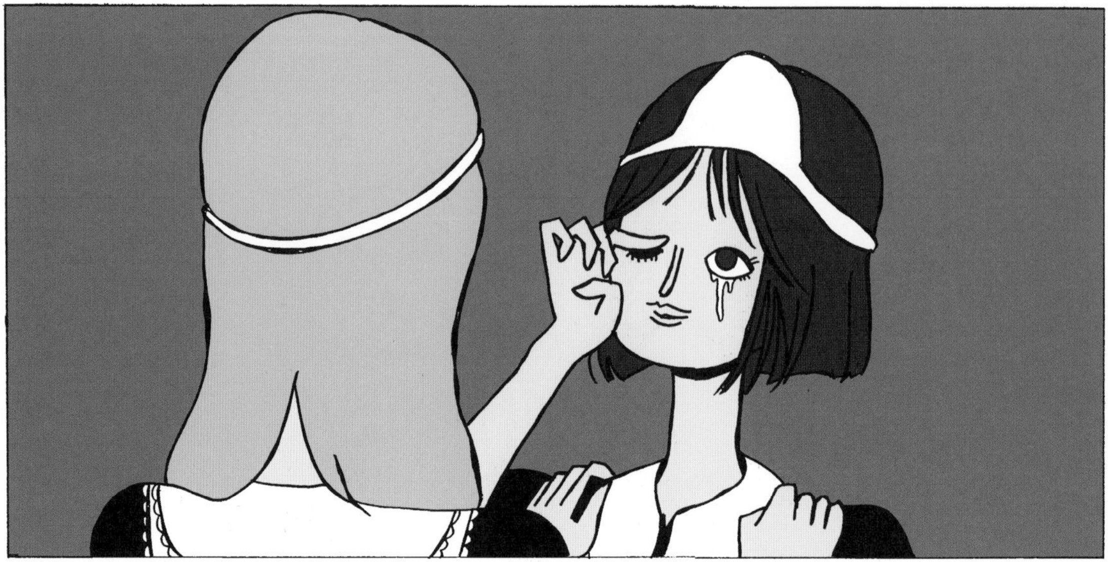

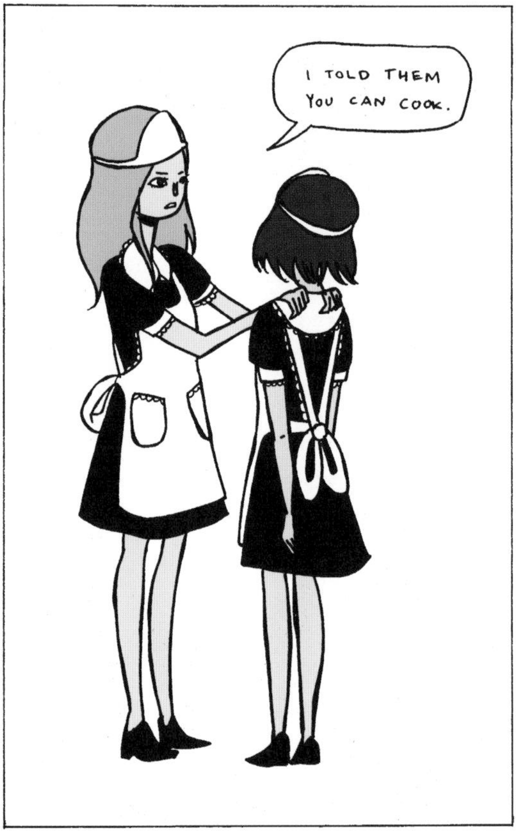
I TOLD THEM YOU CAN COOK.

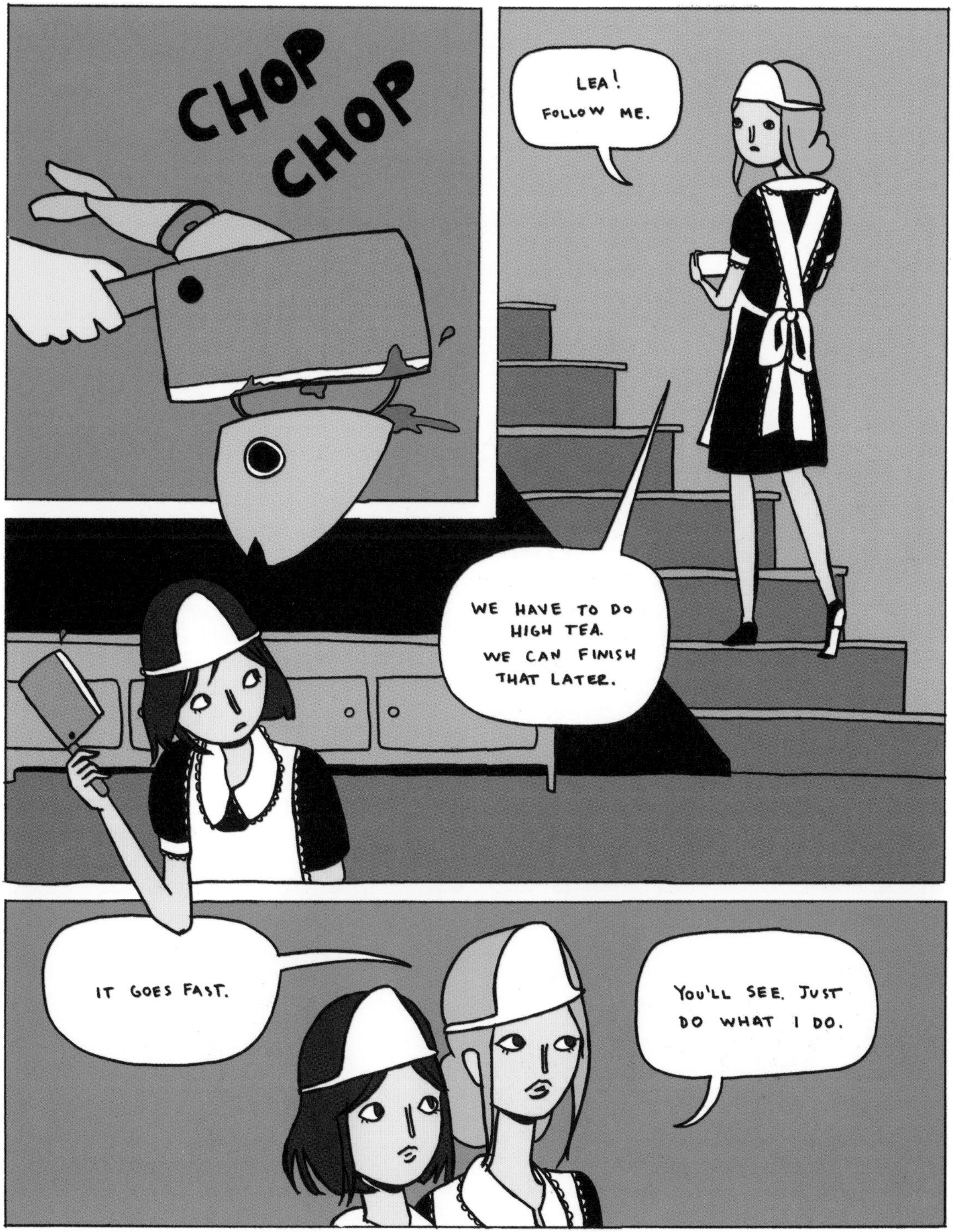
CHOP CHOP
LEA! FOLLOW ME.
WE HAVE TO DO HIGH TEA. WE CAN FINISH THAT LATER.
IT GOES FAST.
YOU'LL SEE. JUST DO WHAT I DO.

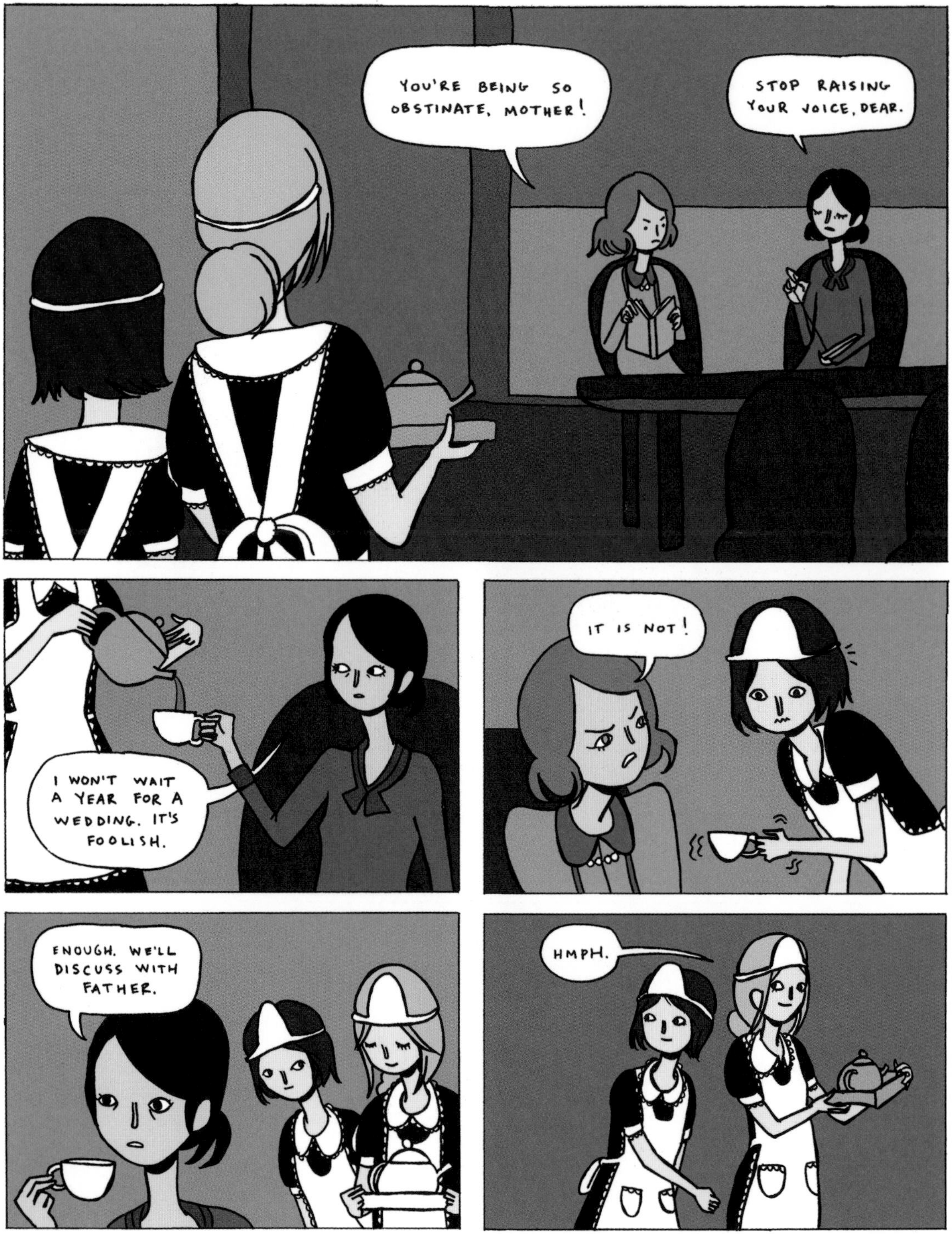
YOU'RE BEING SO OBSTINATE, MOTHER!
STOP RAISING YOUR VOICE, DEAR.
I WON'T WAIT A YEAR FOR A WEDDING. IT'S FOOLISH.
IT IS NOT!
ENOUGH. WE'LL DISCUSS WITH FATHER.
HMPH.

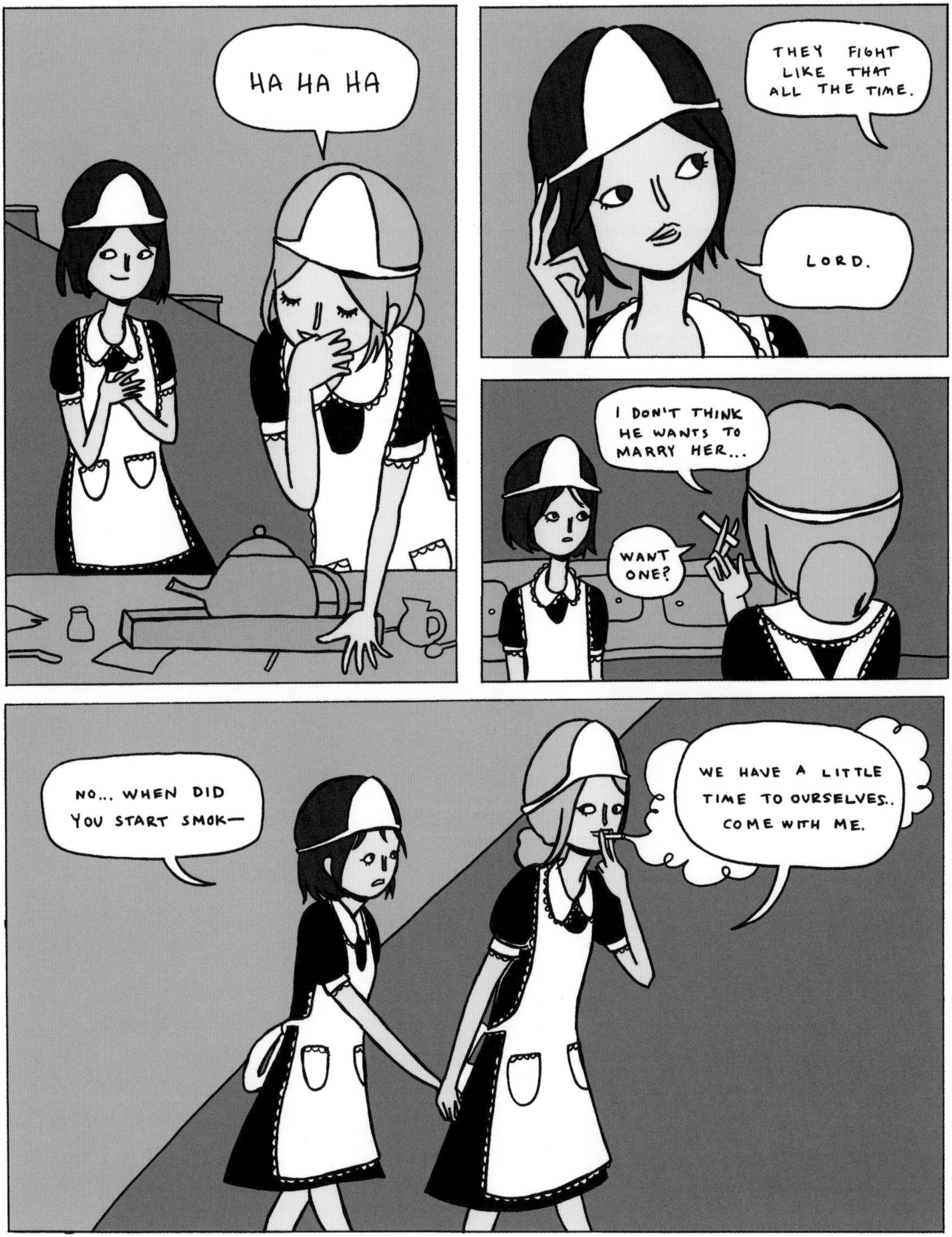
HA HA HA
THEY FIGHT LIKE THAT ALL THE TIME.
LORD.
I DON'T THINK HE WANTS TO MARRY HER...
WANT ONE?
NO... WHEN DID YOU START SMOK—
WE HAVE A LITTLE TIME TO OURSELVES.. COME WITH ME.

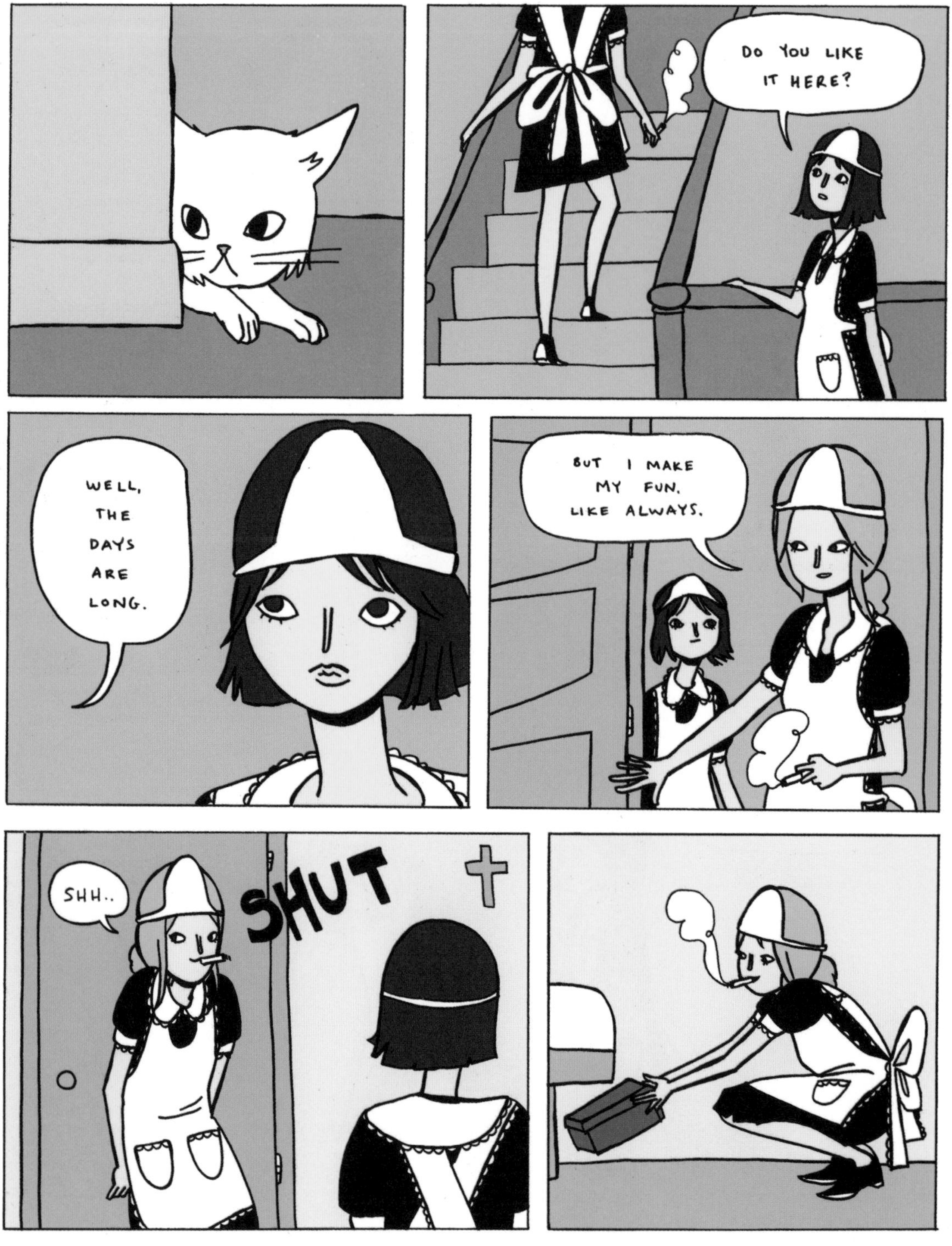
DO YOU LIKE IT HERE?
WELL, THE DAYS ARE LONG.
BUT I MAKE MY FUN. LIKE ALWAYS.
SHH..
SHUT

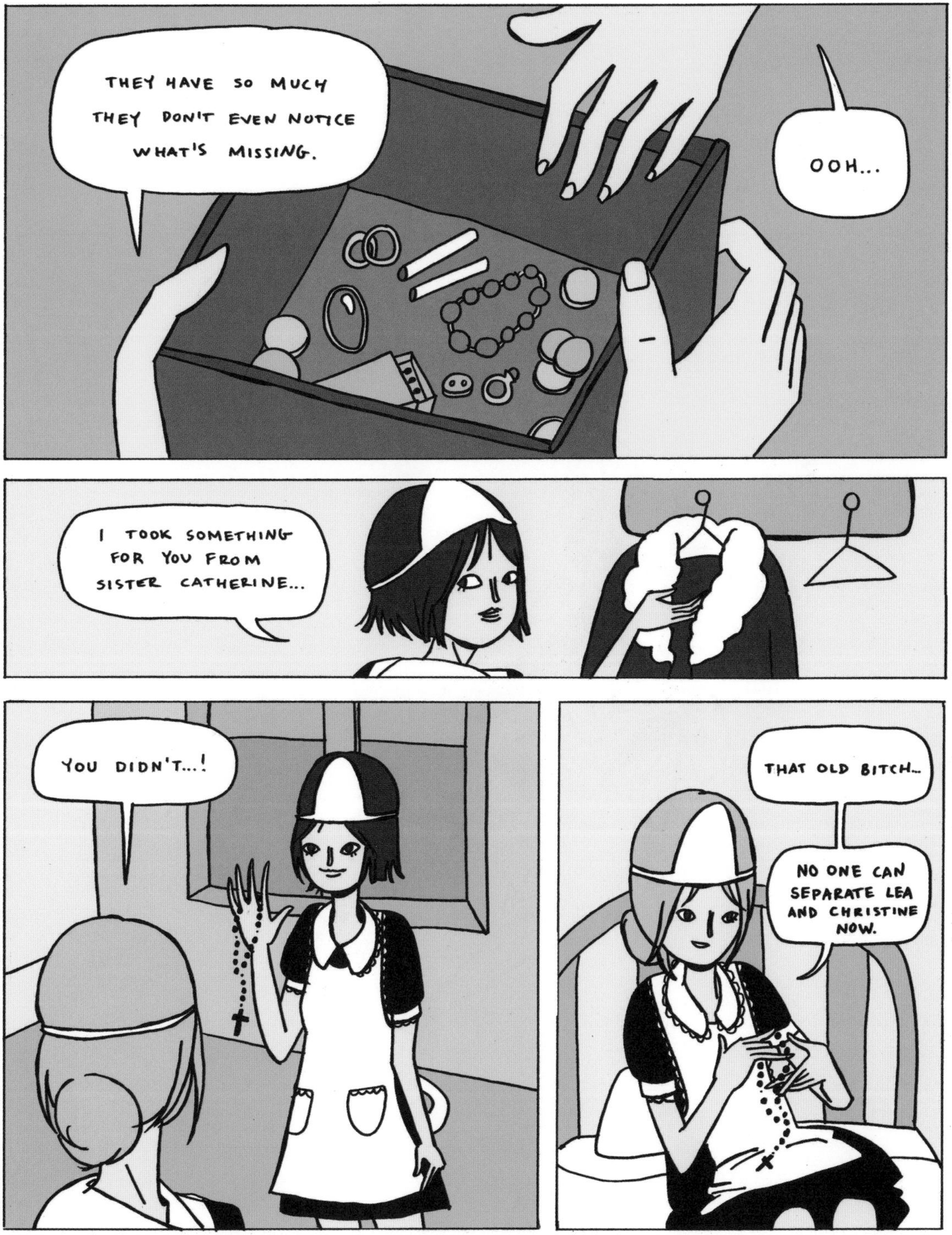
THEY HAVE SO MUCH THEY DON'T EVEN NOTICE WHAT'S MISSING.
OOH...
I TOOK SOMETHING FOR YOU FROM SISTER CATHERINE...
YOU DIDN'T...!
THAT OLD BITCH...
NO ONE CAN SEPARATE LEA AND CHRISTINE NOW.

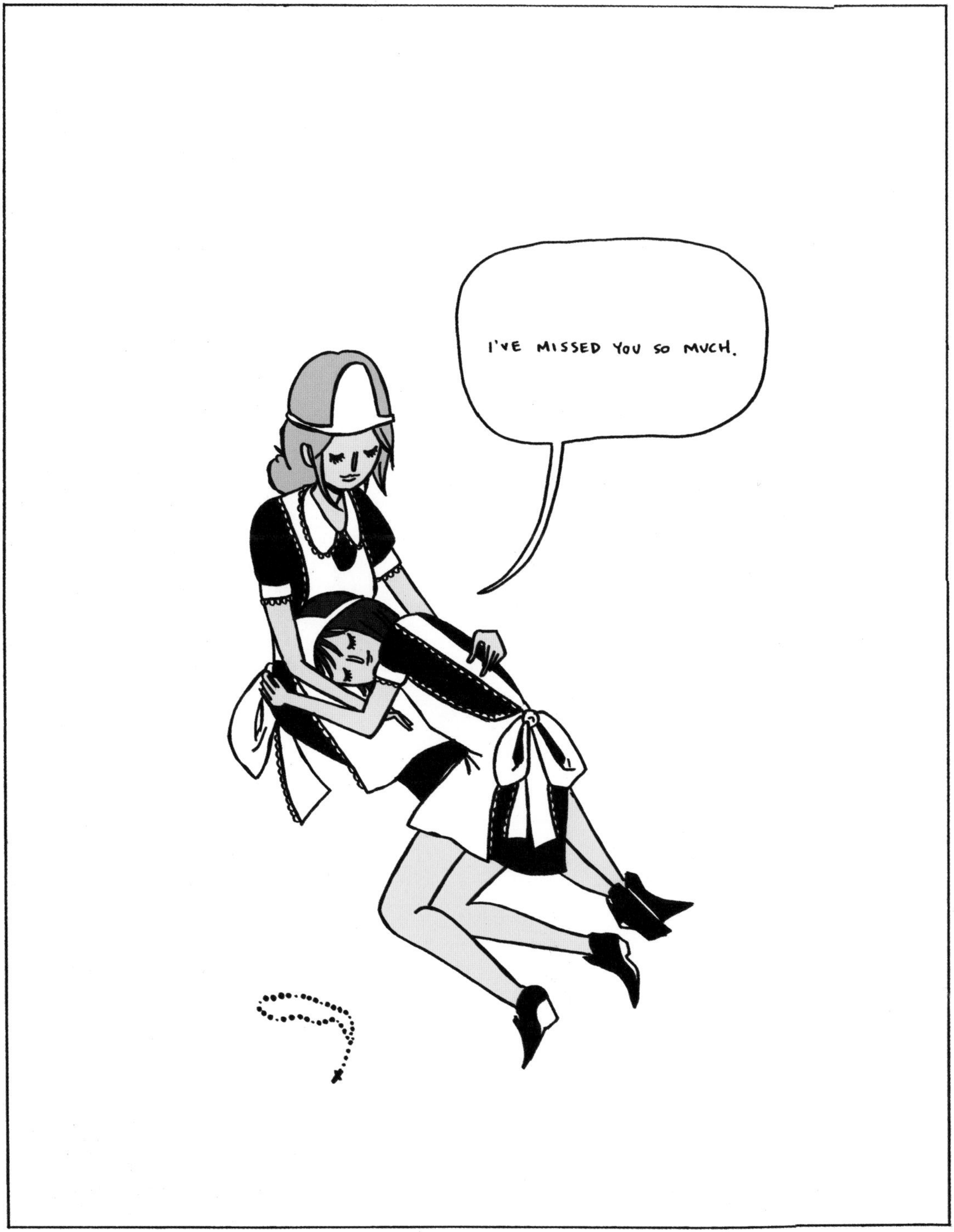
I'VE MISSED YOU SO MUCH.

CHAPTER

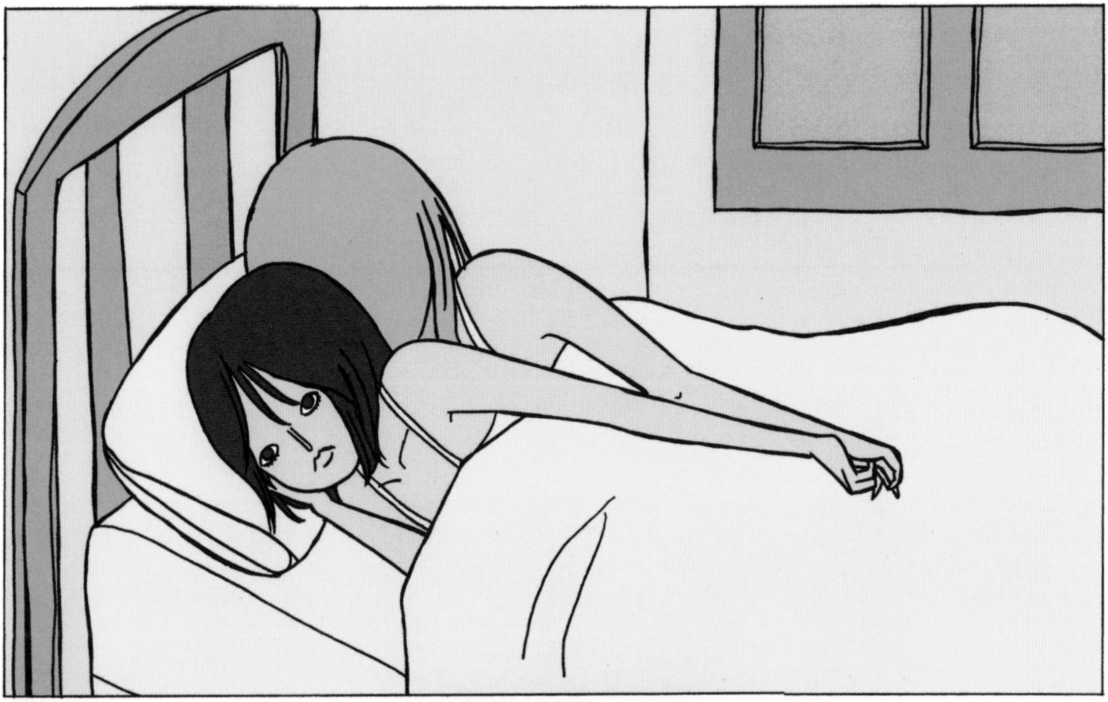

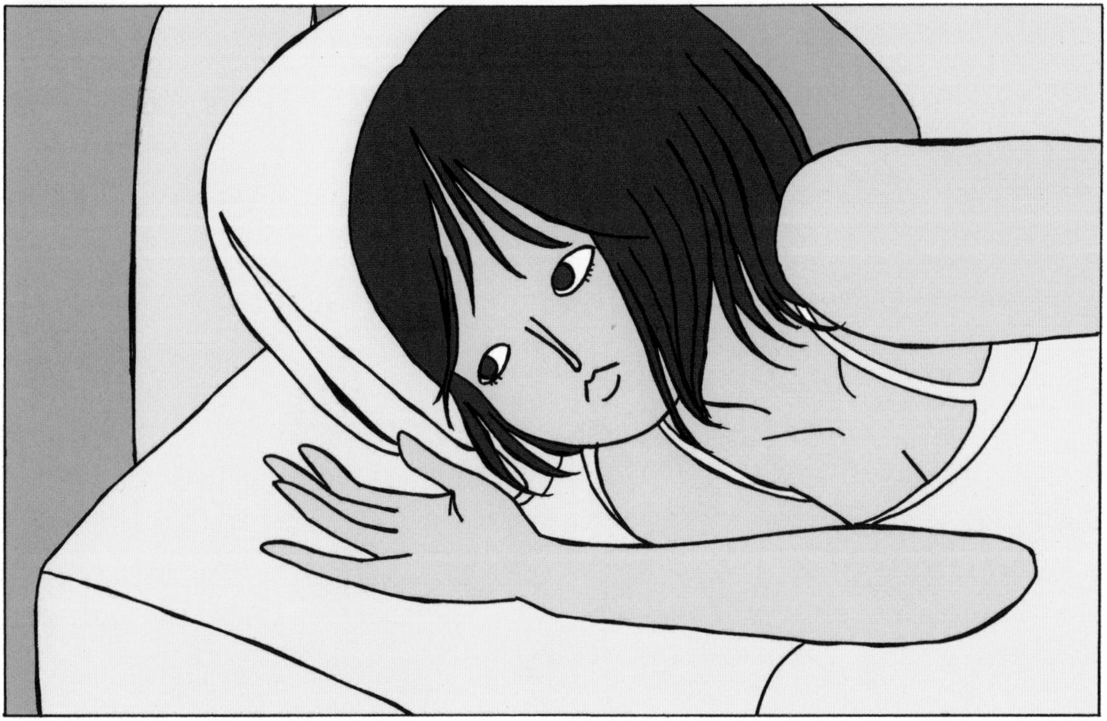

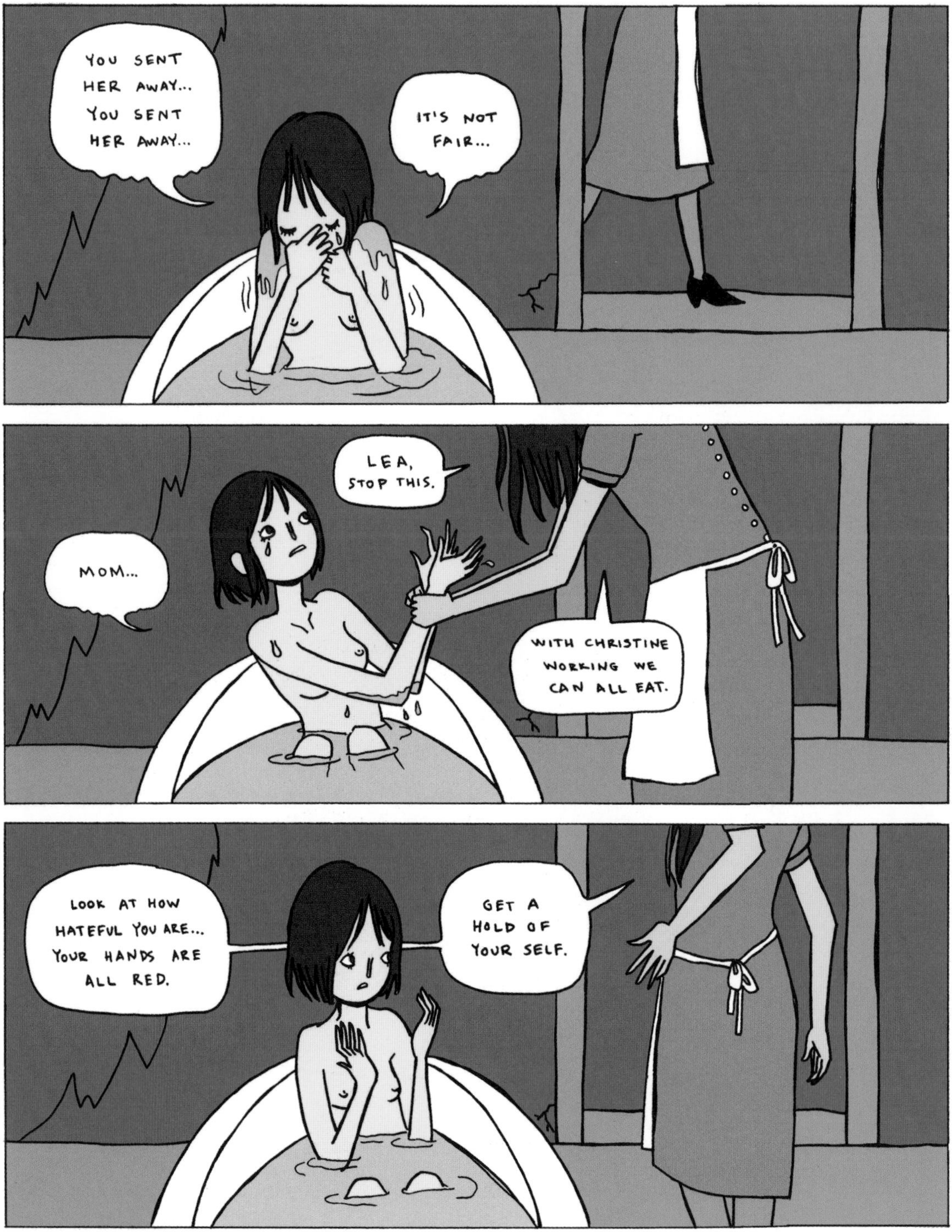
YOU SENT HER AWAY... YOU SENT HER AWAY...
IT'S NOT FAIR...
LEA, STOP THIS.
MOM...
WITH CHRISTINE WORKING WE CAN ALL EAT.
LOOK AT HOW HATEFUL YOU ARE... YOUR HANDS ARE ALL RED.
GET A HOLD OF YOUR SELF.

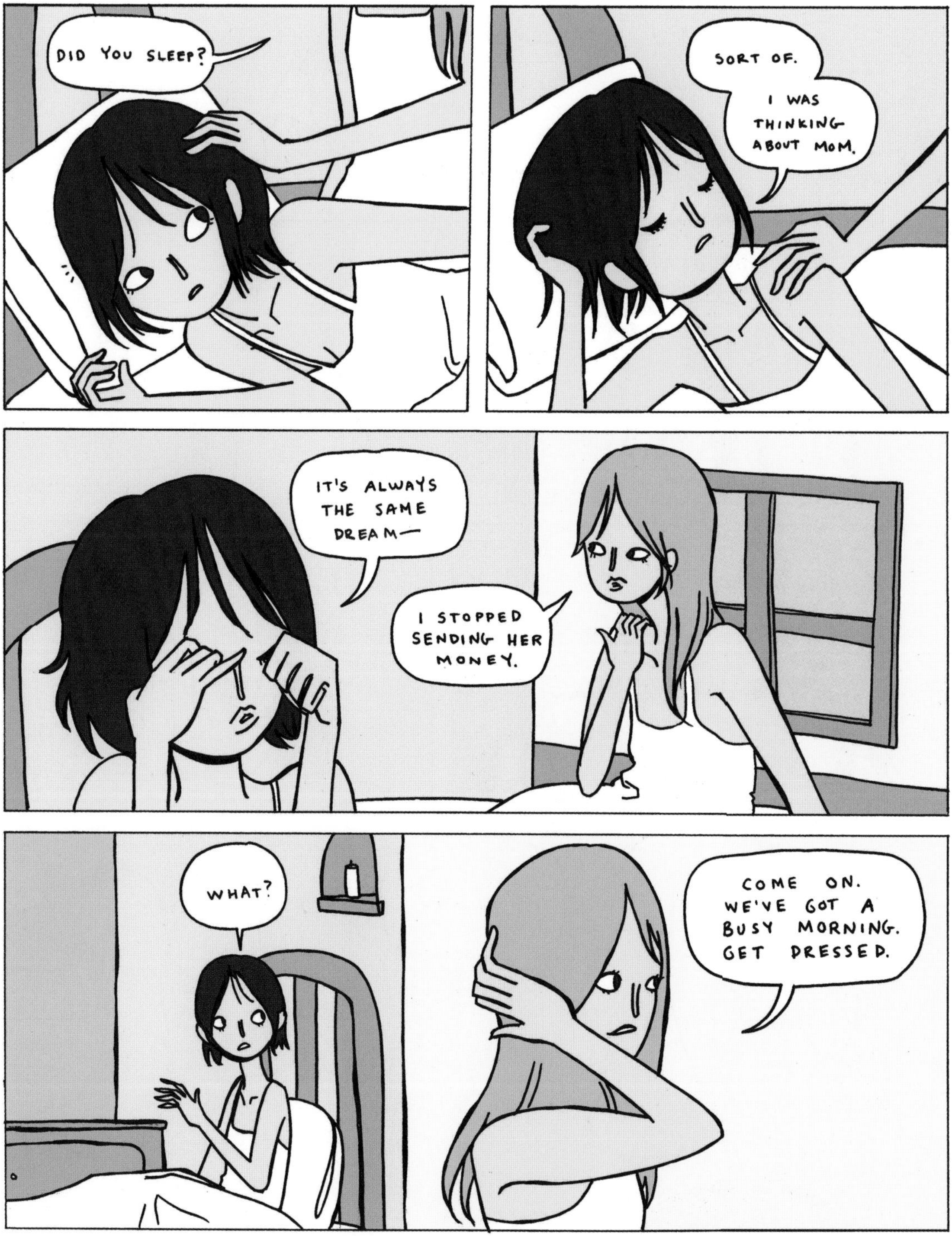
DID YOU SLEEP?
SORT OF.
I WAS THINKING ABOUT MOM.
IT'S ALWAYS THE SAME DREAM—
I STOPPED SENDING HER MONEY.
WHAT?
COME ON. WE'VE GOT A BUSY MORNING. GET DRESSED.

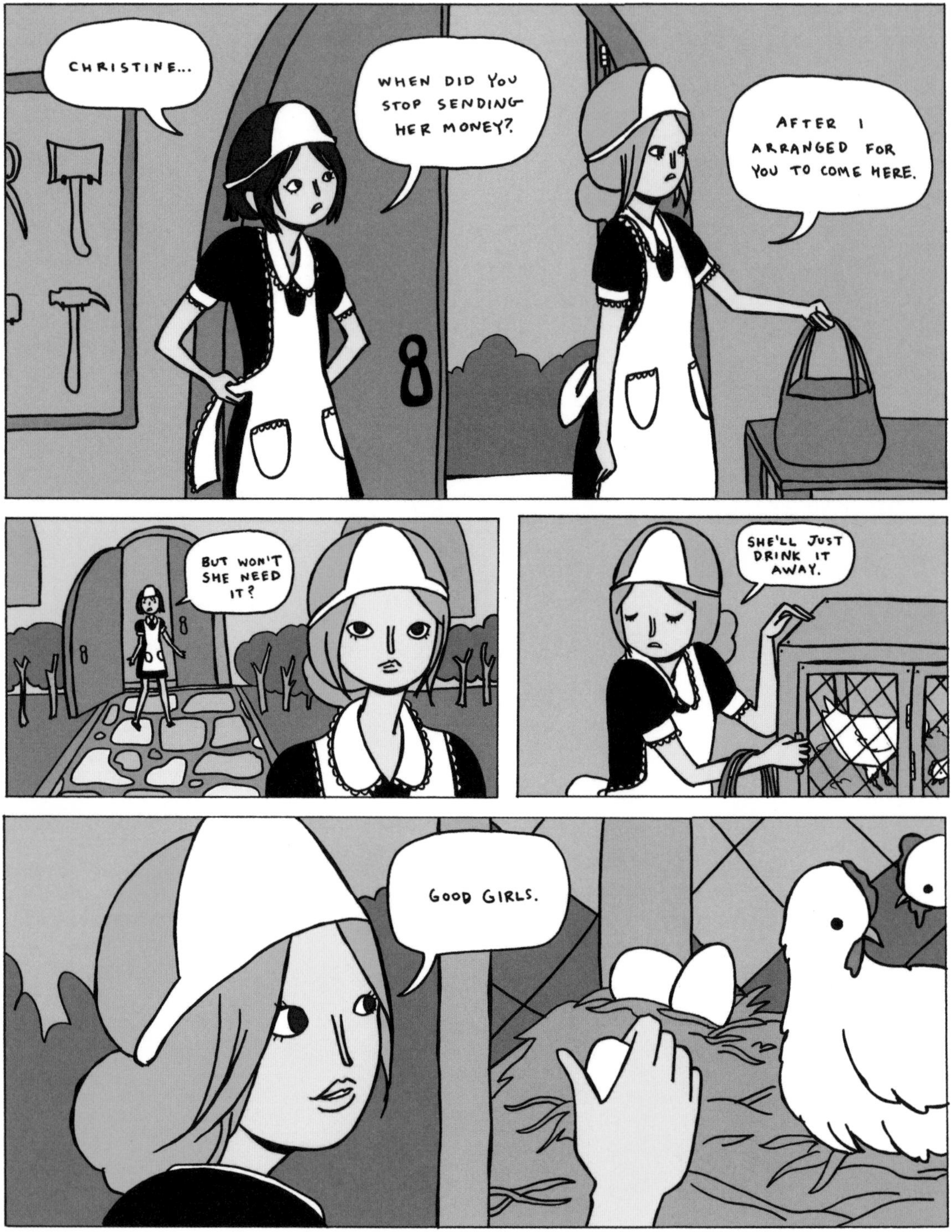
CHRISTINE...
WHEN DID YOU STOP SENDING HER MONEY?
AFTER I ARRANGED FOR YOU TO COME HERE.
BUT WON'T SHE NEED IT?
SHE'LL JUST DRINK IT AWAY.
GOOD GIRLS.

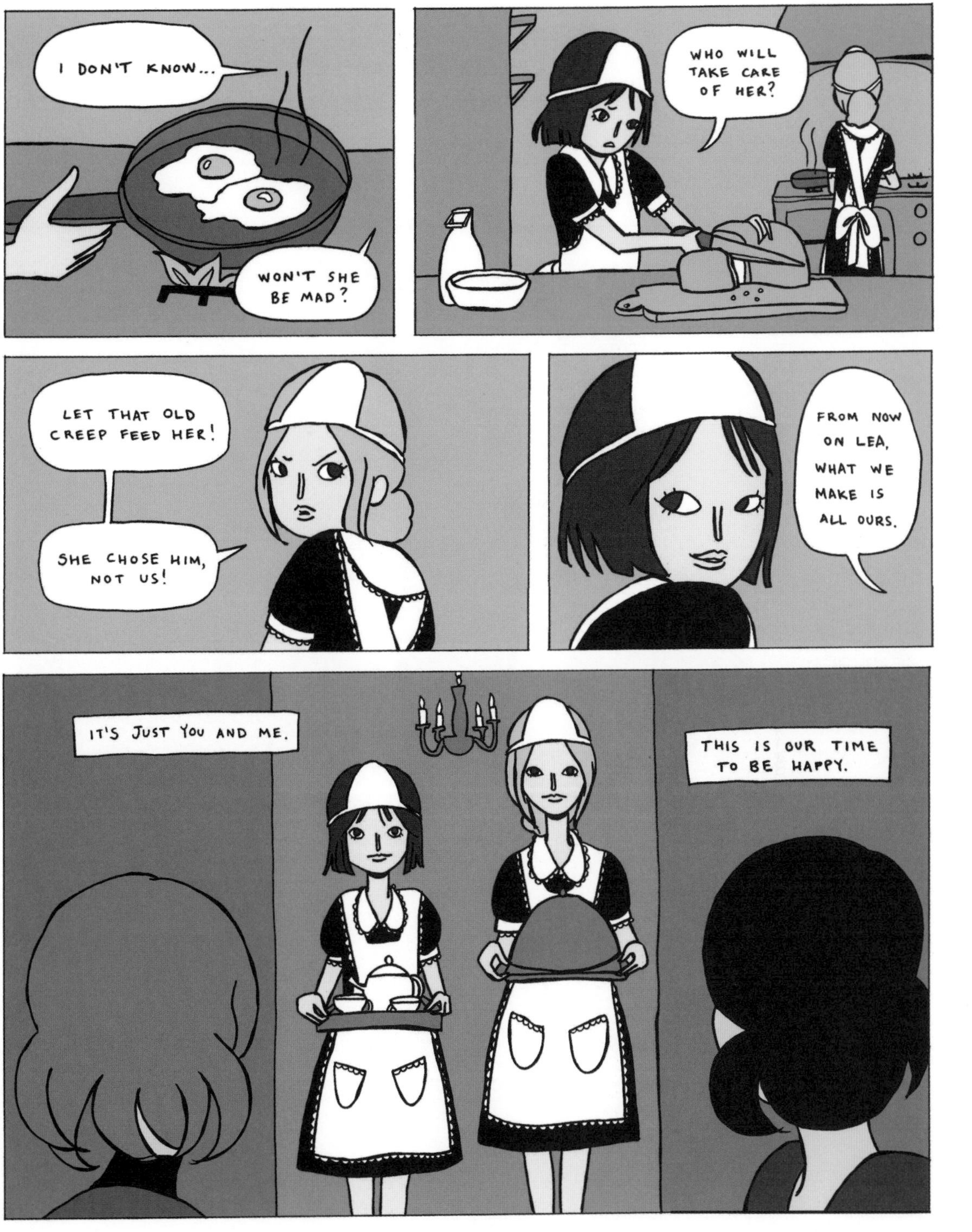
I DON'T KNOW...
WON'T SHE BE MAD?
WHO WILL TAKE CARE OF HER?
LET THAT OLD CREEP FEED HER!
SHE CHOSE HIM, NOT US!
FROM NOW ON LEA, WHAT WE MAKE IS ALL OURS.
IT'S JUST YOU AND ME.
THIS IS OUR TIME TO BE HAPPY.

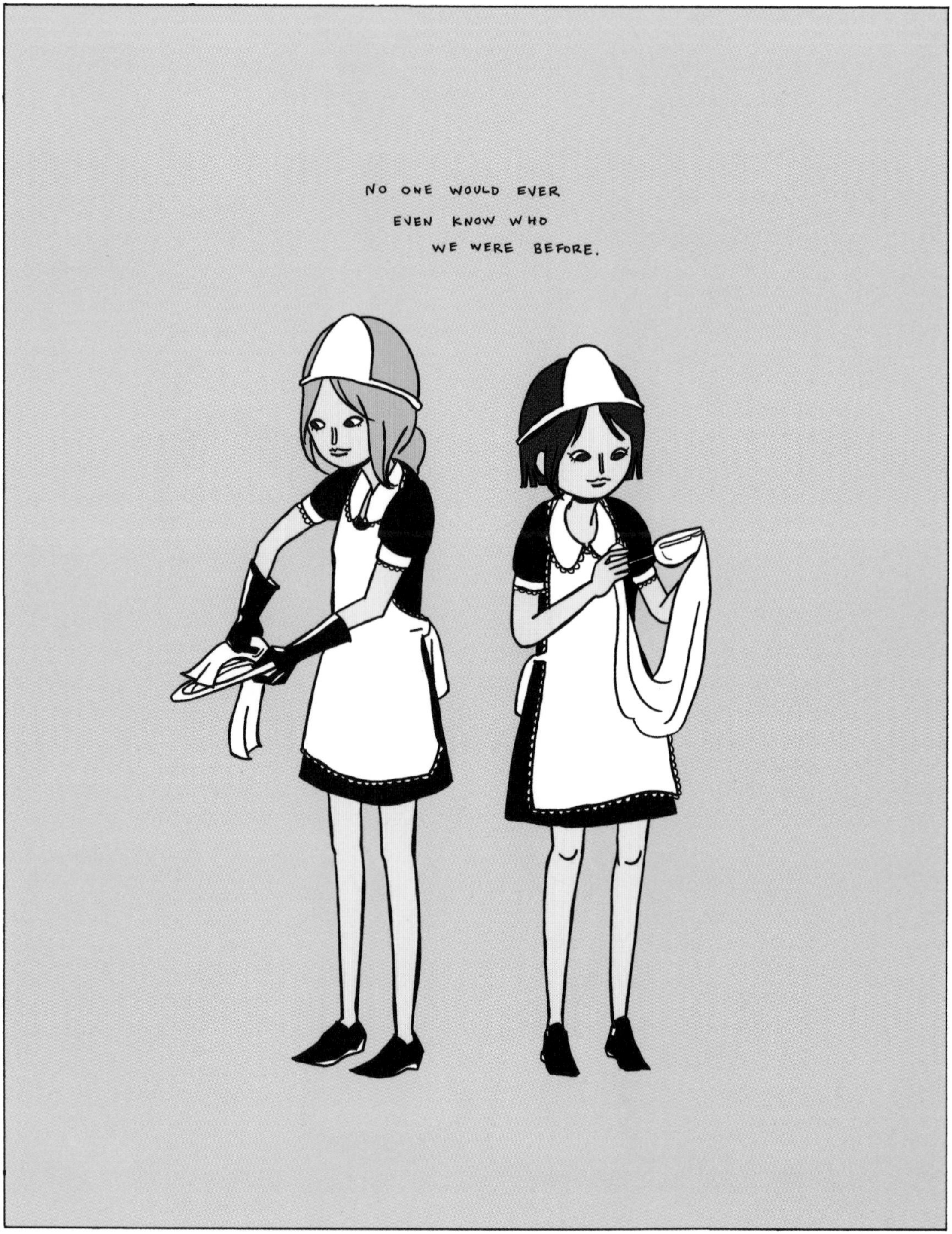
NO ONE WOULD EVER
EVEN KNOW WHO
WE WERE BEFORE.

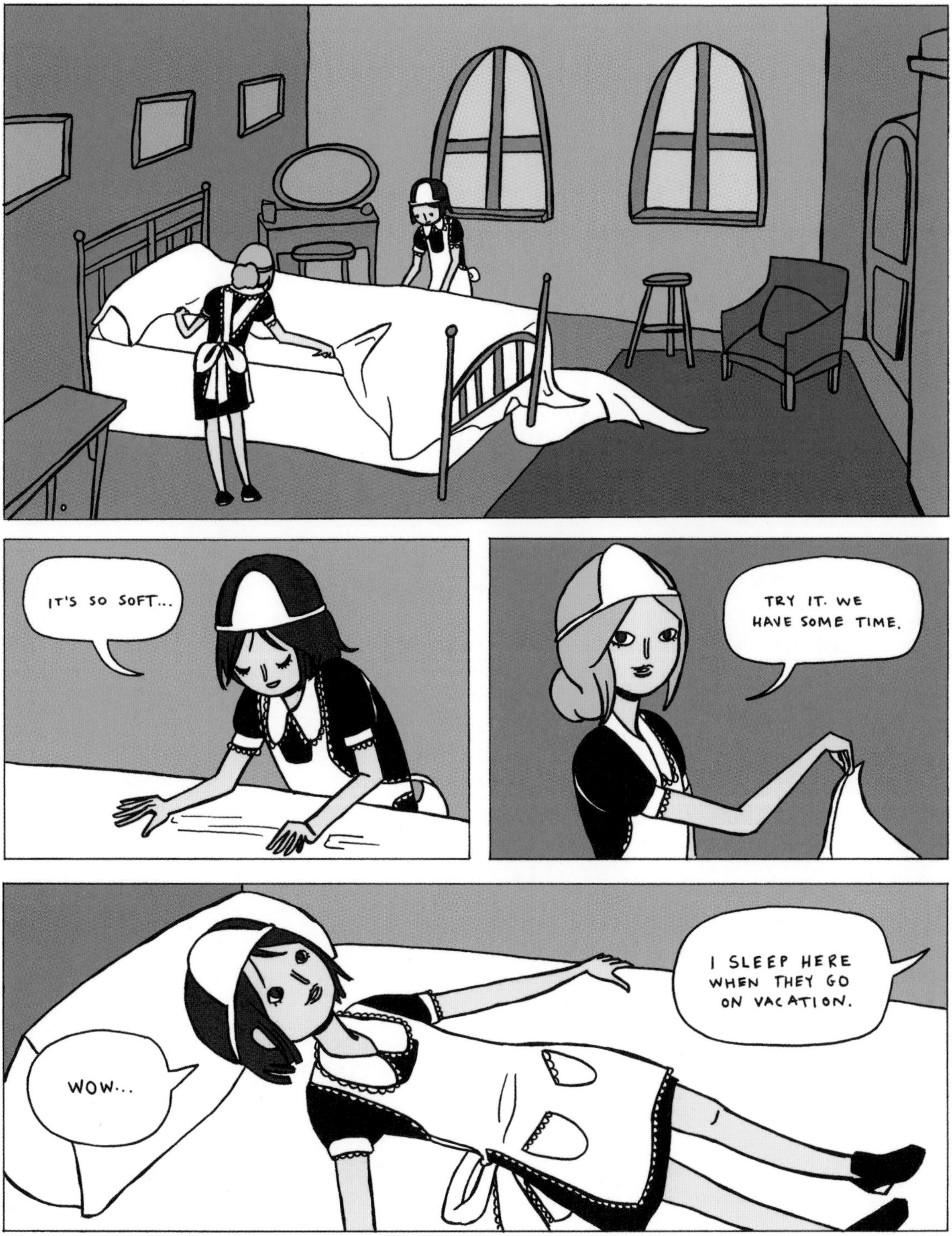
IT'S SO SOFT...
TRY IT. WE HAVE SOME TIME.
I SLEEP HERE WHEN THEY GO ON VACATION.
WOW...

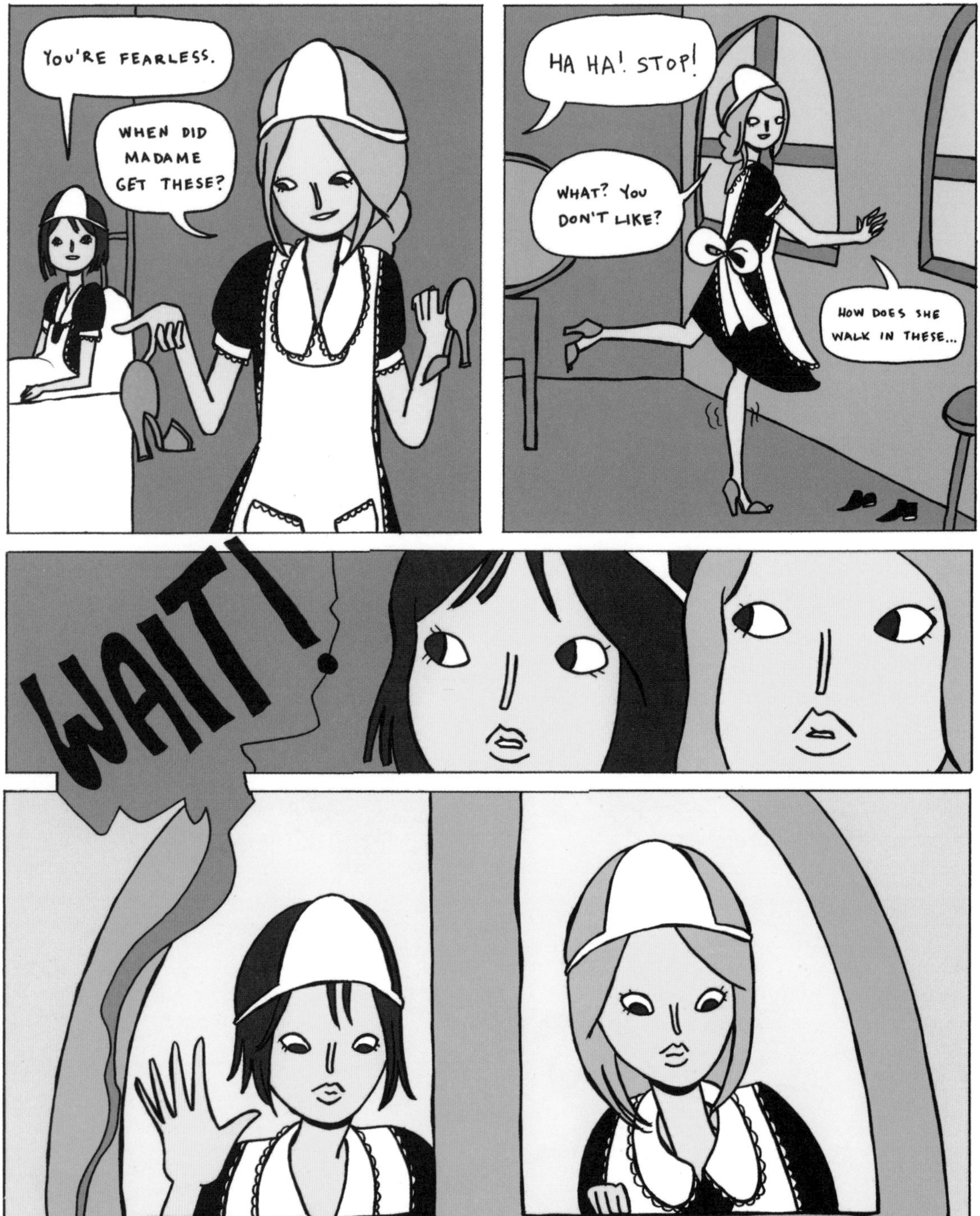
YOU'RE FEARLESS.
WHEN DID MADAME GET THESE?
HA HA! STOP!
WHAT? YOU DON'T LIKE?
HOW DOES SHE WALK IN THESE...
WAIT!

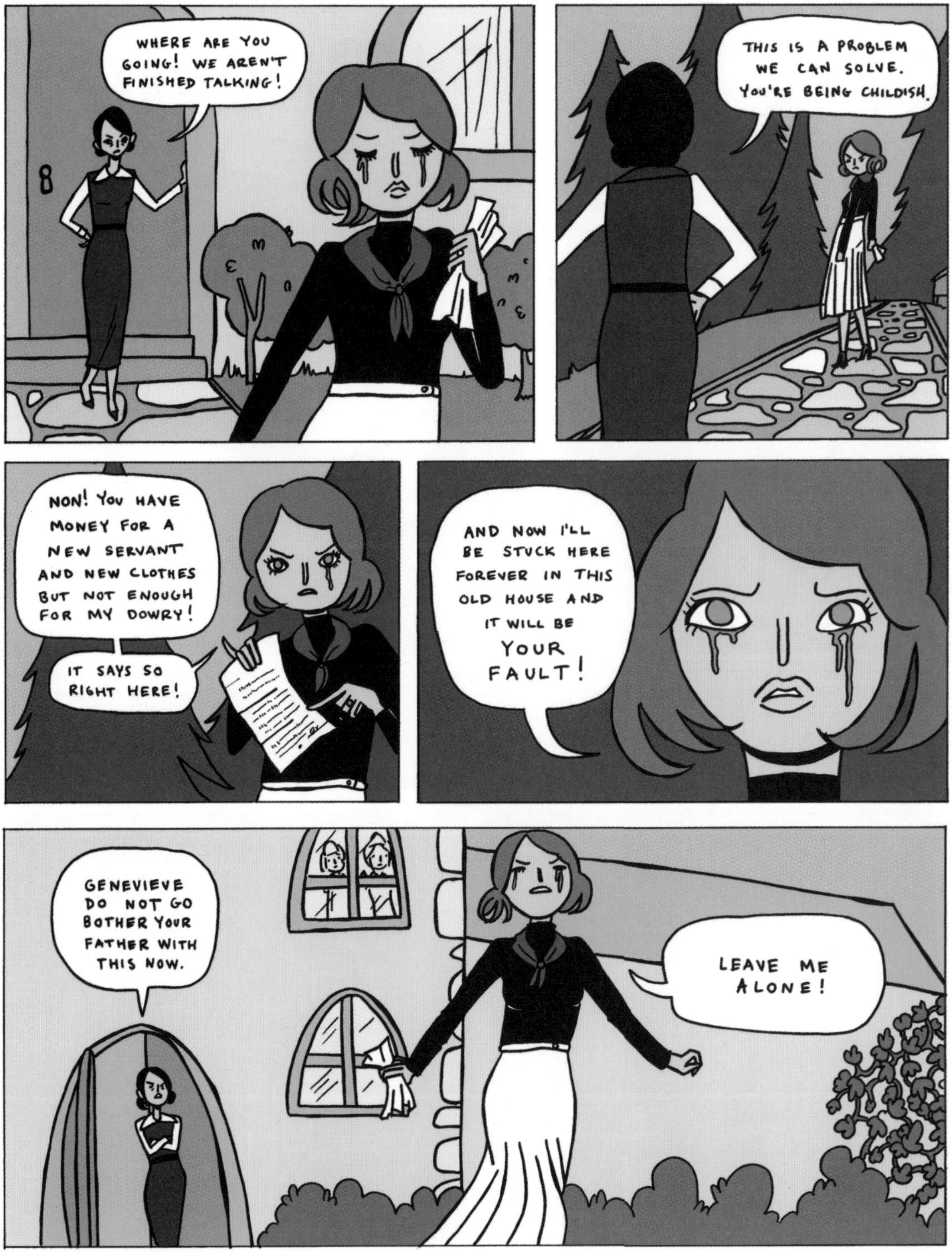
WHERE ARE YOU GOING! WE AREN'T FINISHED TALKING!
THIS IS A PROBLEM WE CAN SOLVE. YOU'RE BEING CHILDISH.
NON! YOU HAVE MONEY FOR A NEW SERVANT AND NEW CLOTHES BUT NOT ENOUGH FOR MY DOWRY!
IT SAYS SO RIGHT HERE!
AND NOW I'LL BE STUCK HERE FOREVER IN THIS OLD HOUSE AND IT WILL BE YOUR FAULT!
GENEVIEVE DO NOT GO BOTHER YOUR FATHER WITH THIS NOW.
LEAVE ME ALONE!

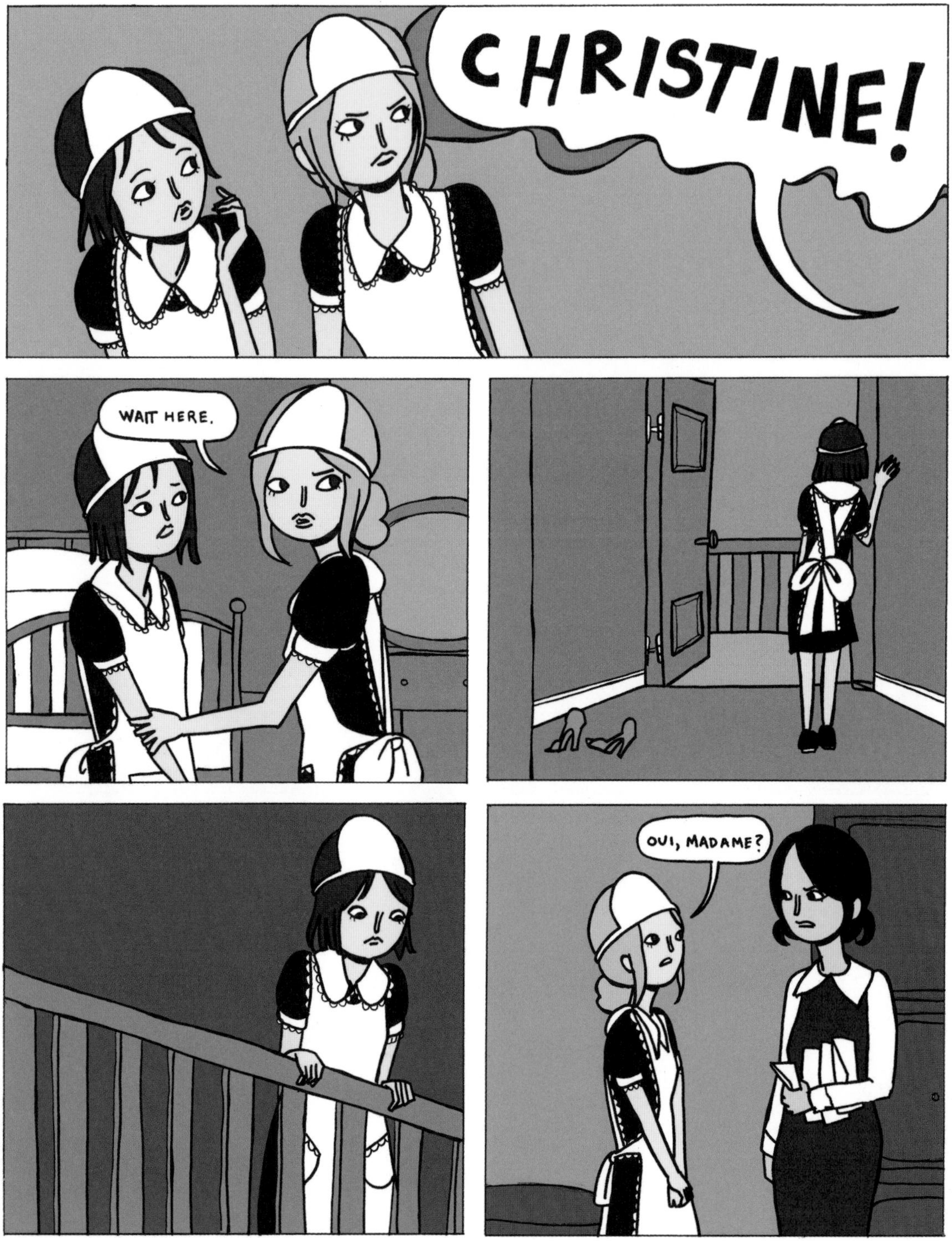
CHRISTINE!
WAIT HERE.
OUI, MADAME?

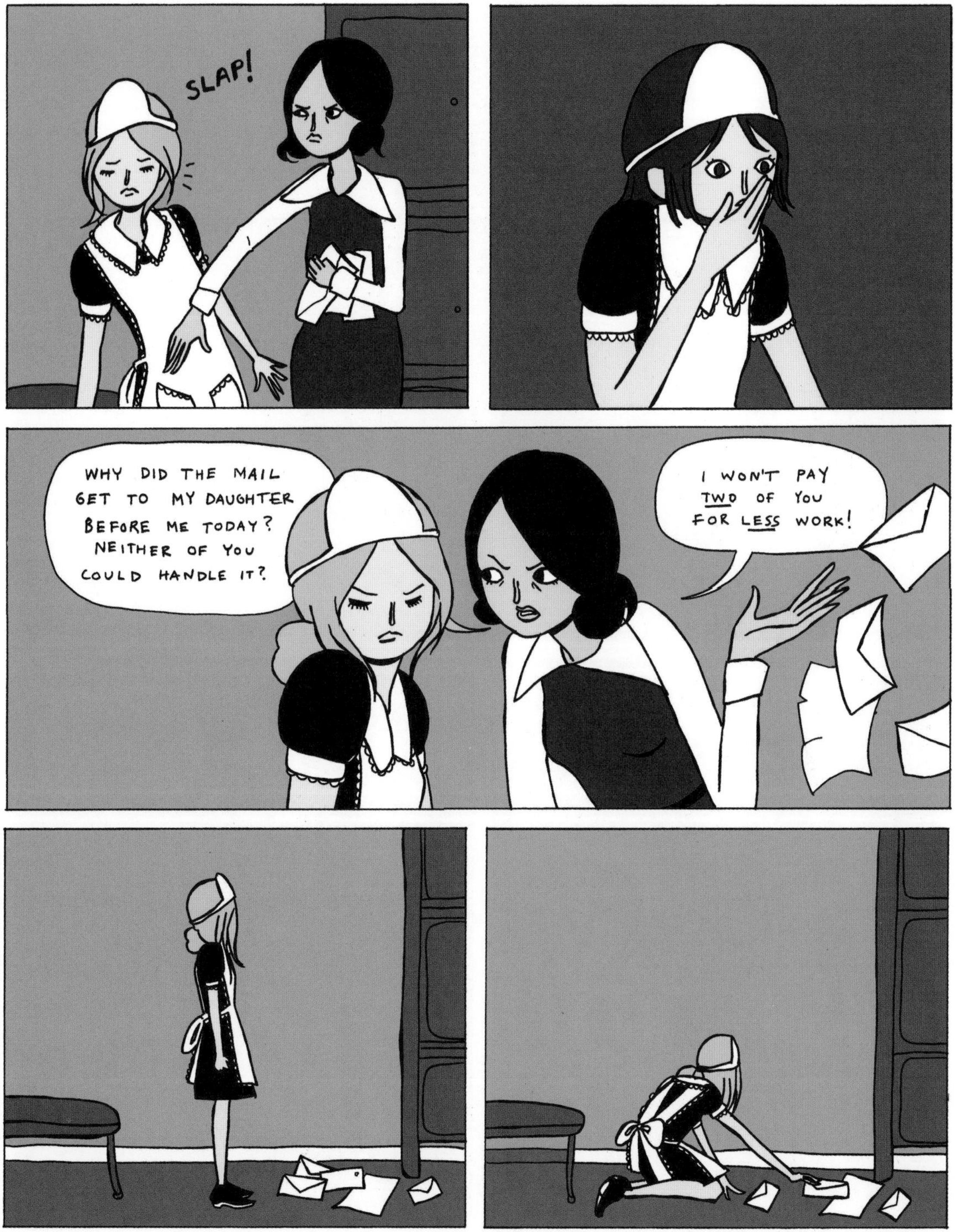
SLAP!
WHY DID THE MAIL GET TO MY DAUGHTER BEFORE ME TODAY? NEITHER OF YOU COULD HANDLE IT?
I WON'T PAY TWO OF YOU FOR LESS WORK!

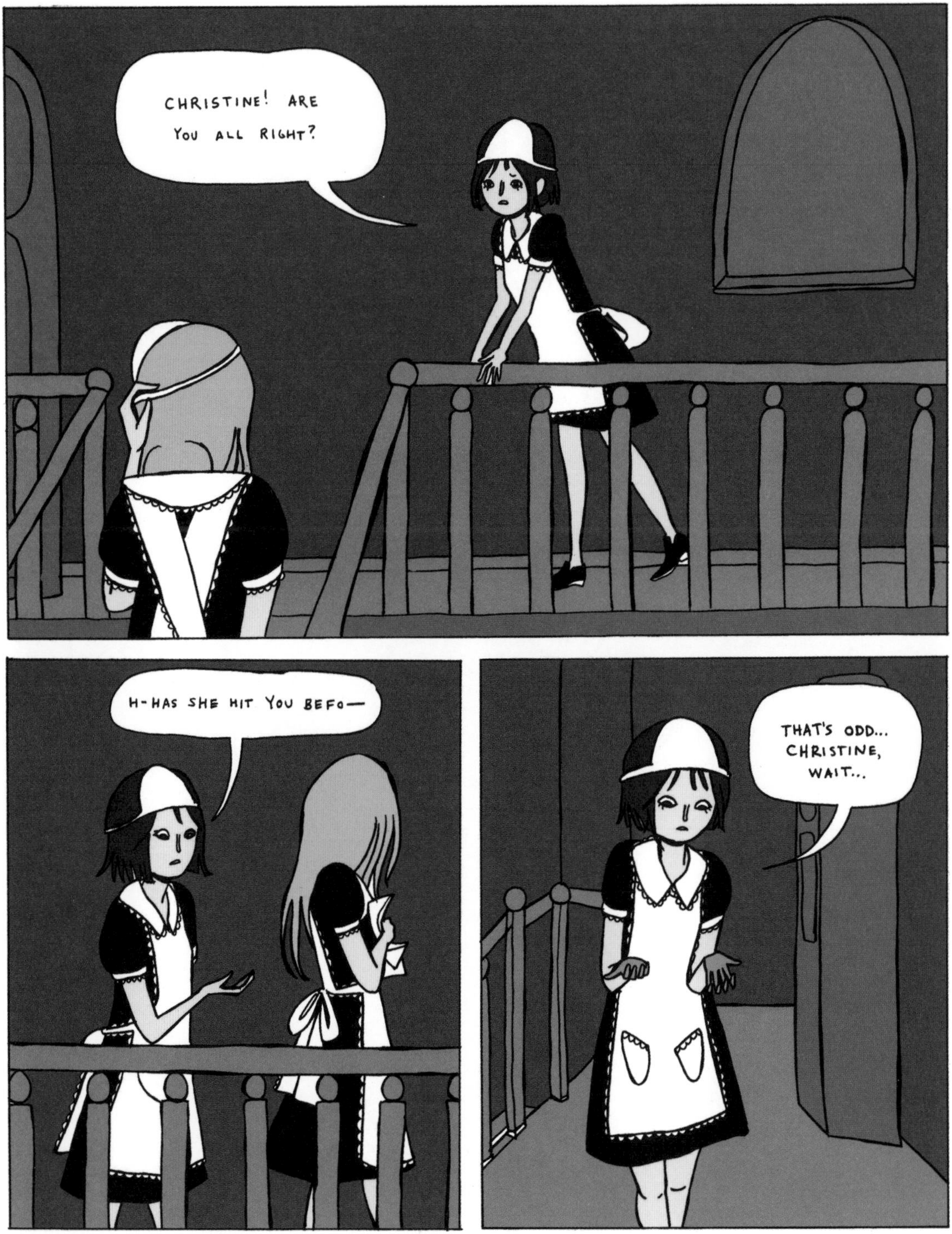
CHRISTINE! ARE YOU ALL RIGHT?
H-HAS SHE HIT YOU BEFO—
THAT'S ODD... CHRISTINE, WAIT...

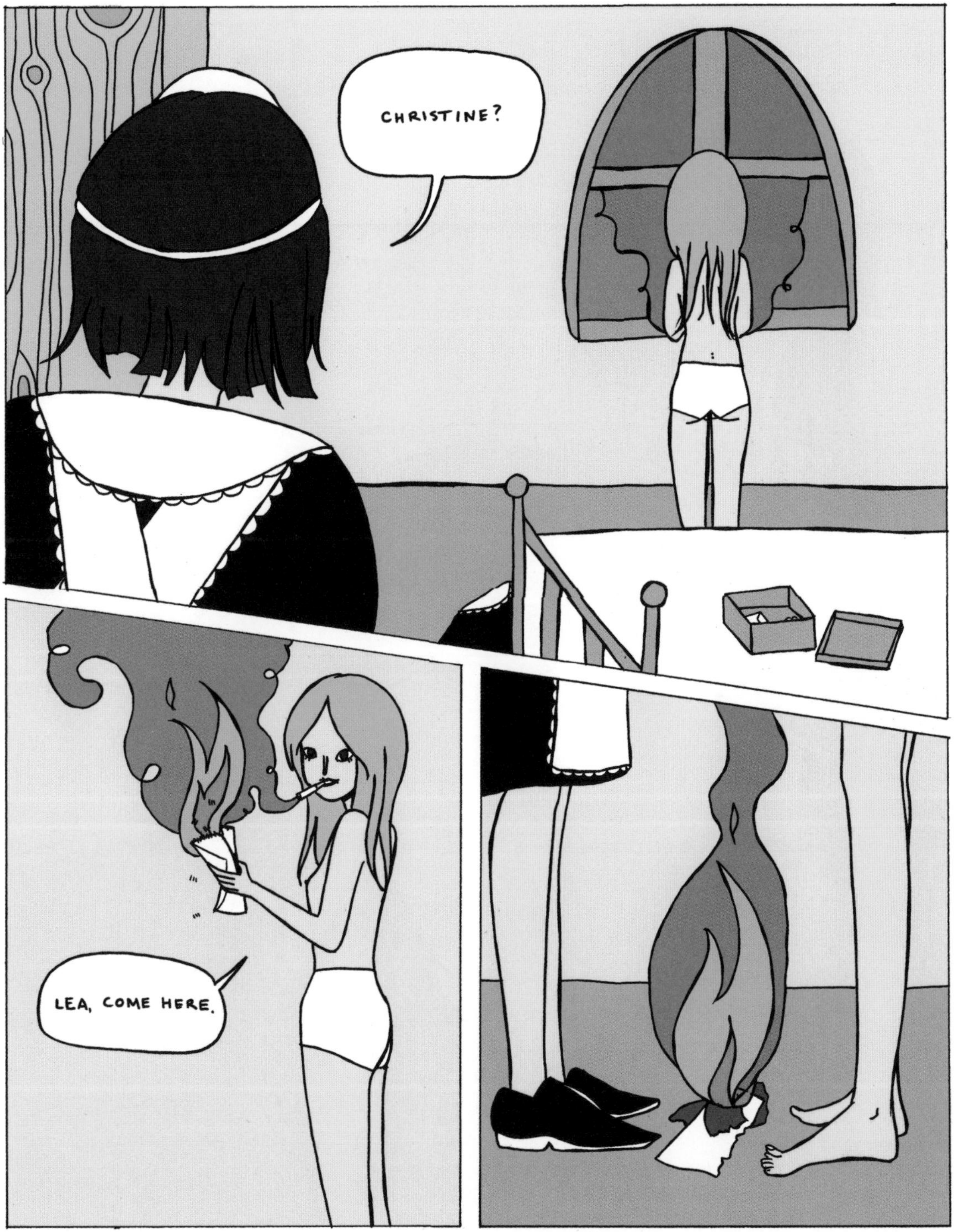
CHRISTINE?
LEA, COME HERE.

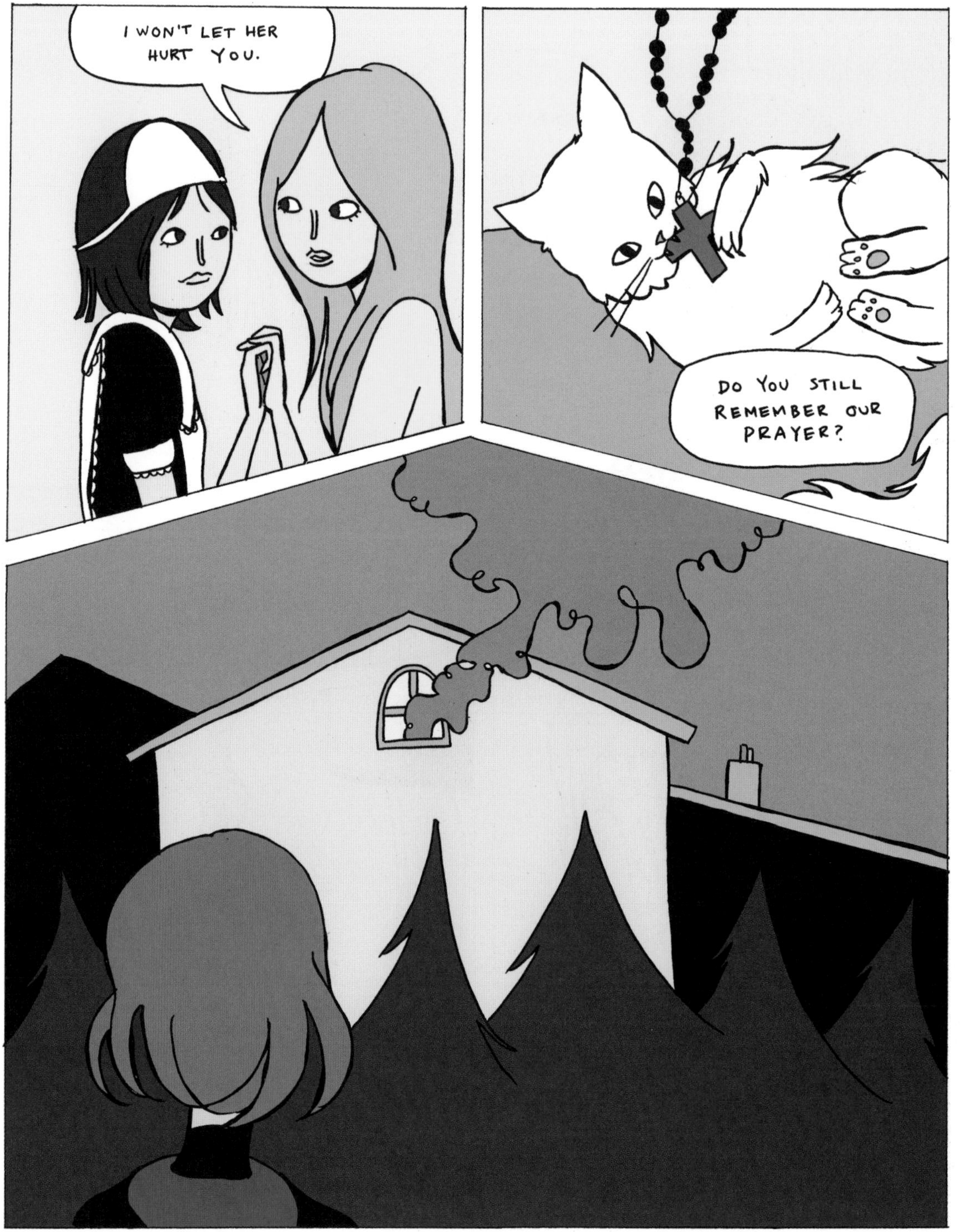
I WON'T LET HER HURT YOU.
DO YOU STILL REMEMBER OUR PRAYER?

CHAPTER

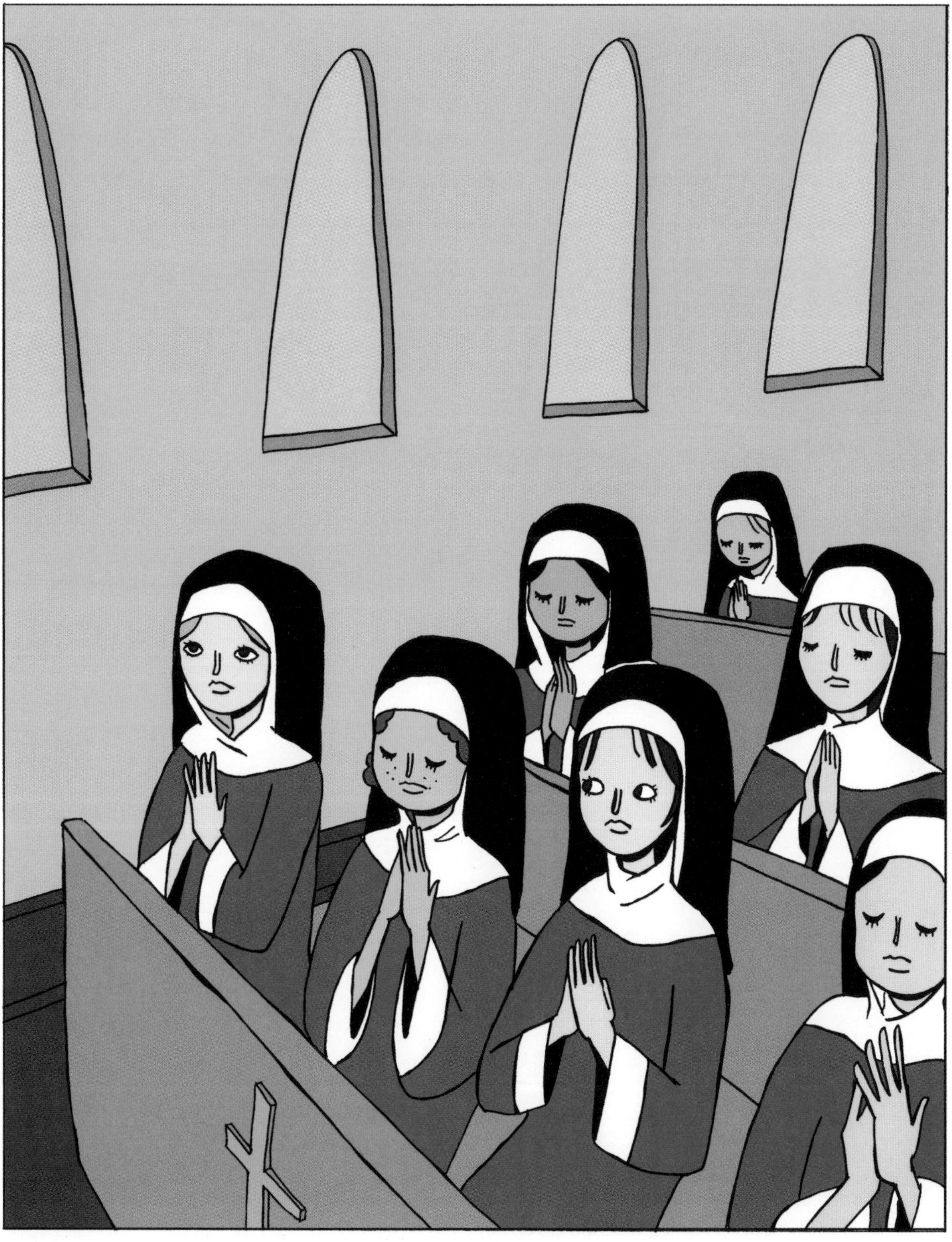

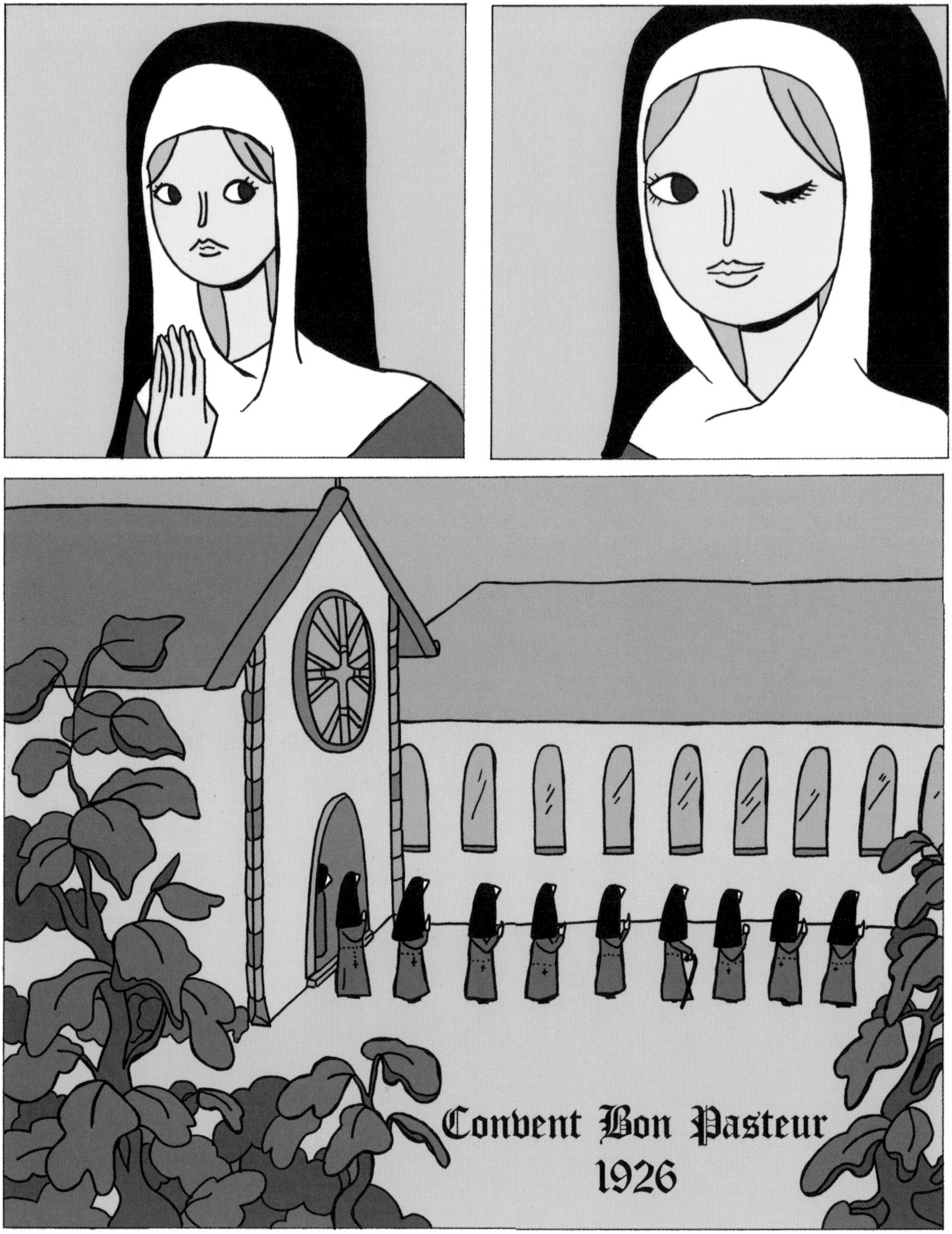
Convent Bon Pasteur
1926

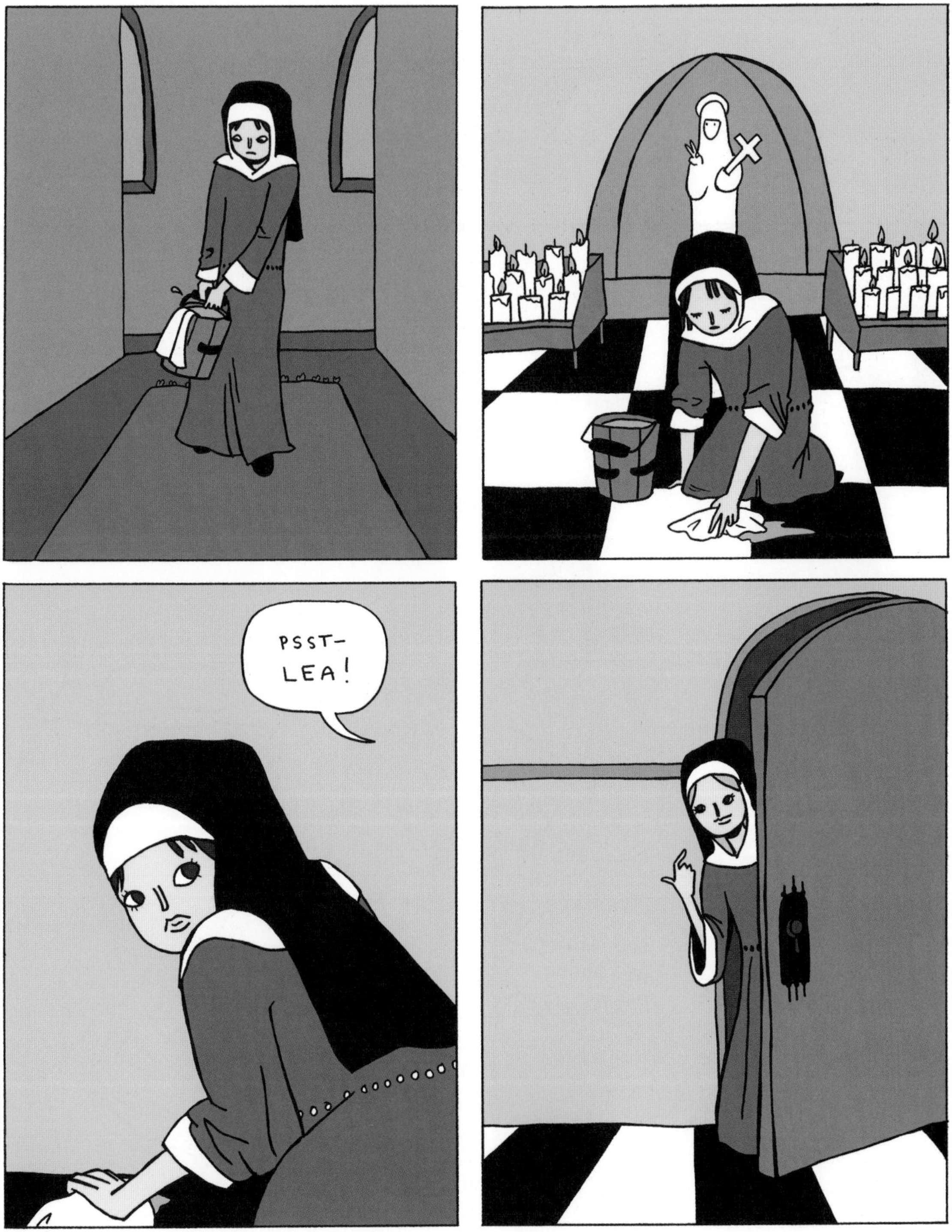
PSST-
LEA!

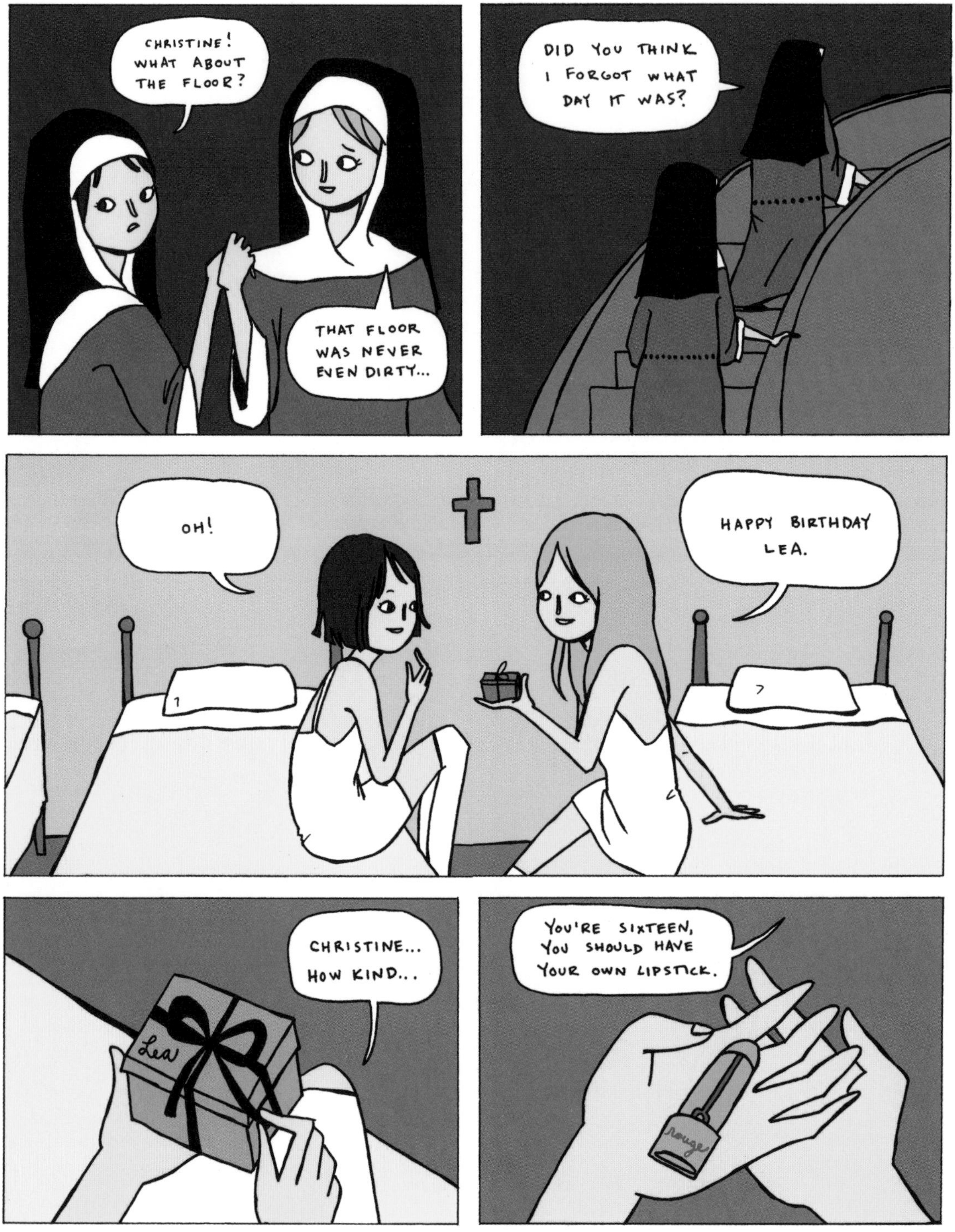
CHRISTINE! WHAT ABOUT THE FLOOR?
THAT FLOOR WAS NEVER EVEN DIRTY...
DID YOU THINK I FORGOT WHAT DAY IT WAS?
OH!
HAPPY BIRTHDAY LEA.
CHRISTINE... HOW KIND...
Lea
YOU'RE SIXTEEN, YOU SHOULD HAVE YOUR OWN LIPSTICK.
rouge

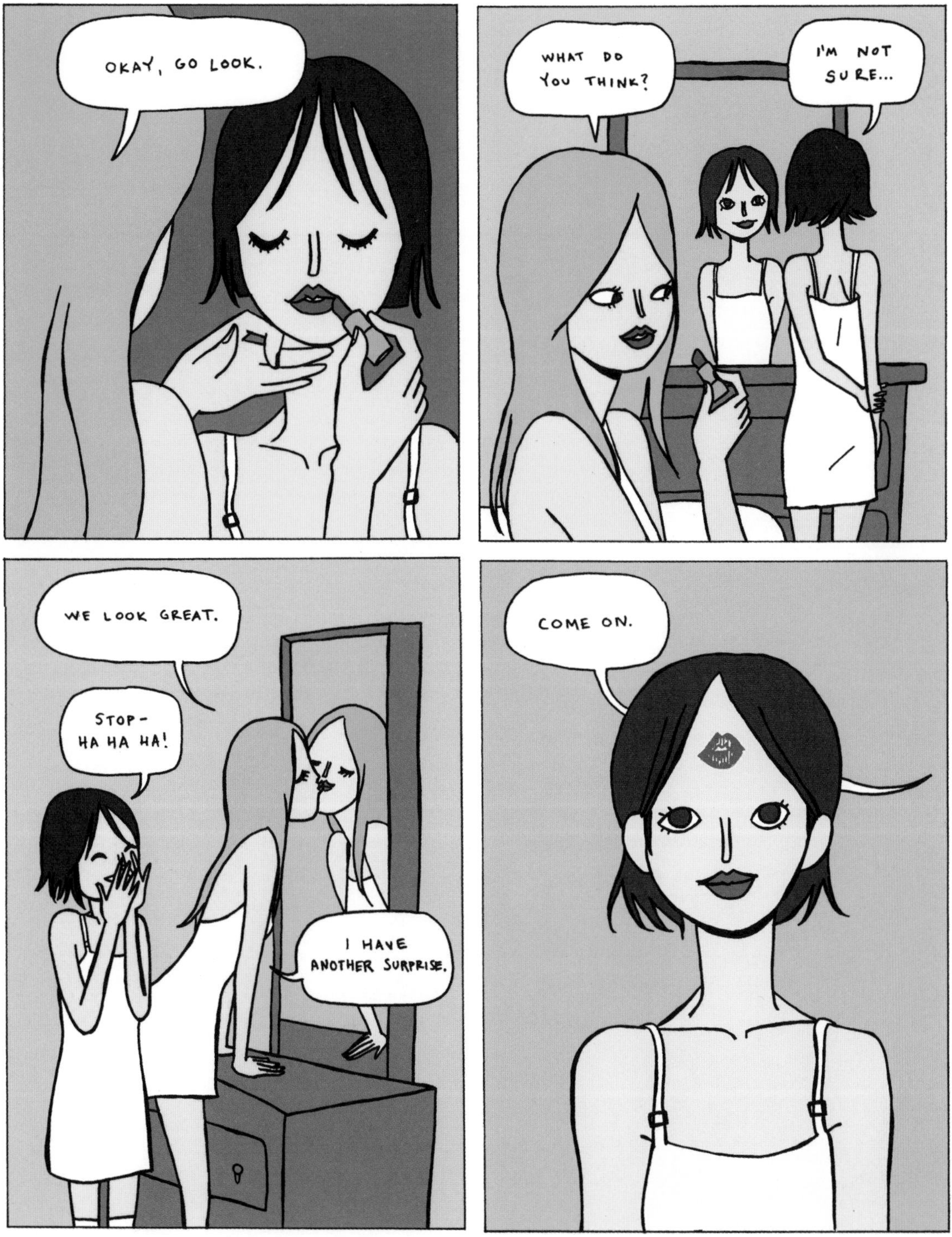
OKAY, GO LOOK.
WHAT DO YOU THINK?
I'M NOT SURE...
WE LOOK GREAT.
STOP- HA HA HA!
I HAVE ANOTHER SURPRISE.
COME ON.

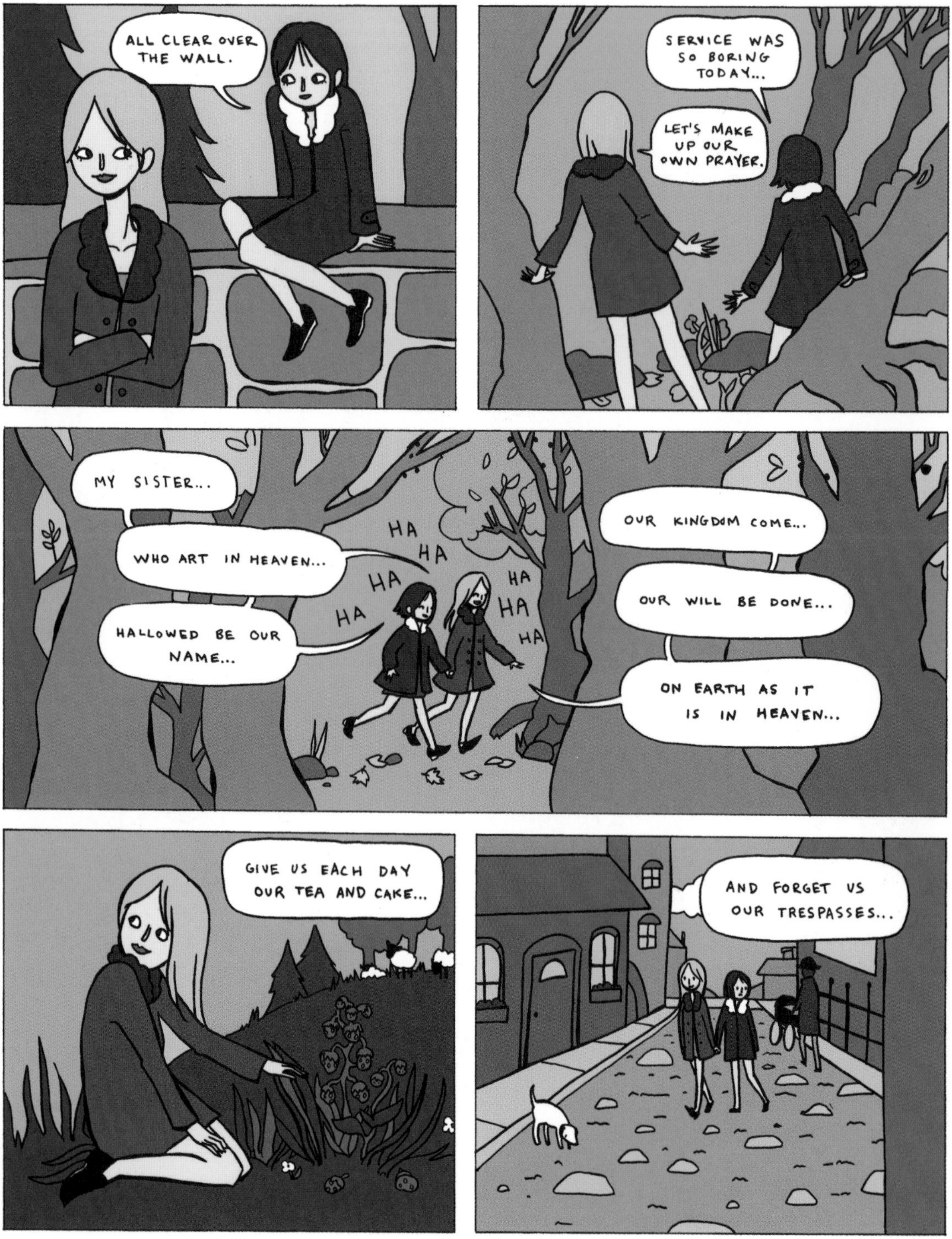
ALL CLEAR OVER THE WALL.
SERVICE WAS SO BORING TODAY...
LET'S MAKE UP OUR OWN PRAYER.
MY SISTER...
WHO ART IN HEAVEN...
HALLOWED BE OUR NAME...
HA HA HA HA HA
HA HA HA
OUR KINGDOM COME...
OUR WILL BE DONE...
ON EARTH AS IT IS IN HEAVEN...
GIVE US EACH DAY OUR TEA AND CAKE...
AND FORGET US OUR TRESPASSES...

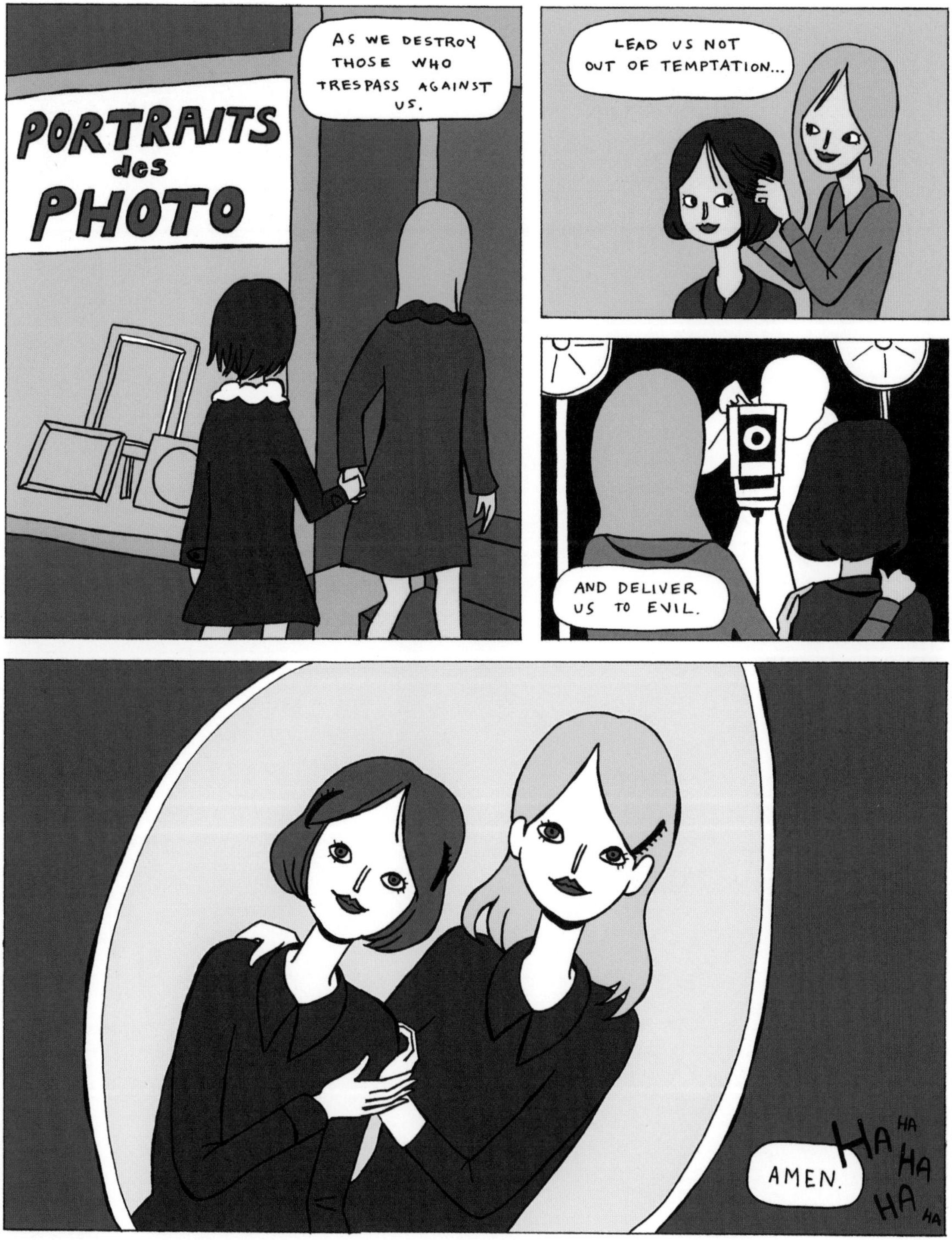
PORTRAITS des PHOTO
AS WE DESTROY THOSE WHO TRESPASS AGAINST US.
LEAD US NOT OUT OF TEMPTATION...
AND DELIVER US TO EVIL.
AMEN.
HA HA HA HA HA

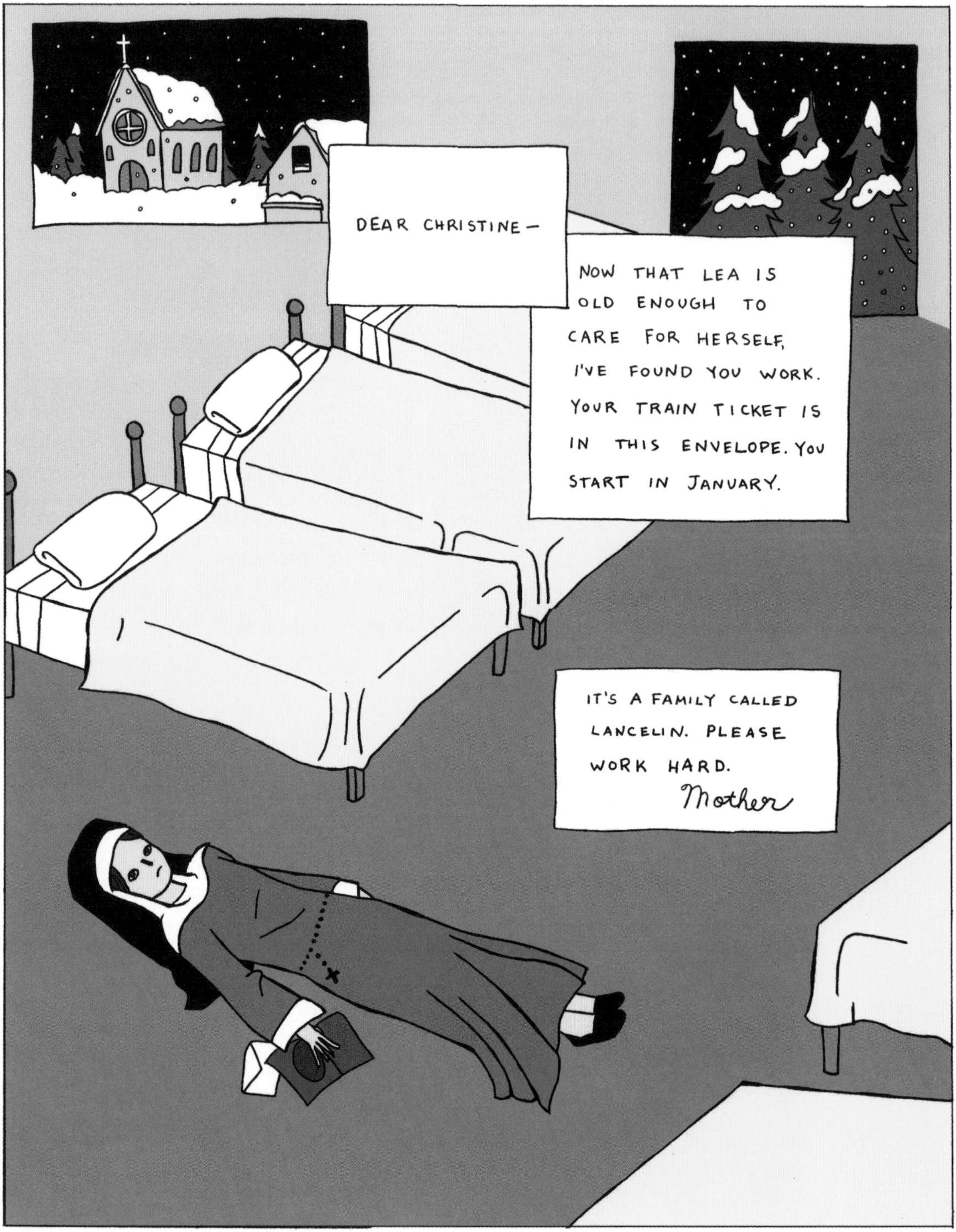
DEAR CHRISTINE—
NOW THAT LEA IS OLD ENOUGH TO CARE FOR HERSELF, I'VE FOUND YOU WORK. YOUR TRAIN TICKET IS IN THIS ENVELOPE. YOU START IN JANUARY.
IT'S A FAMILY CALLED LANCELIN. PLEASE WORK HARD.
Mother

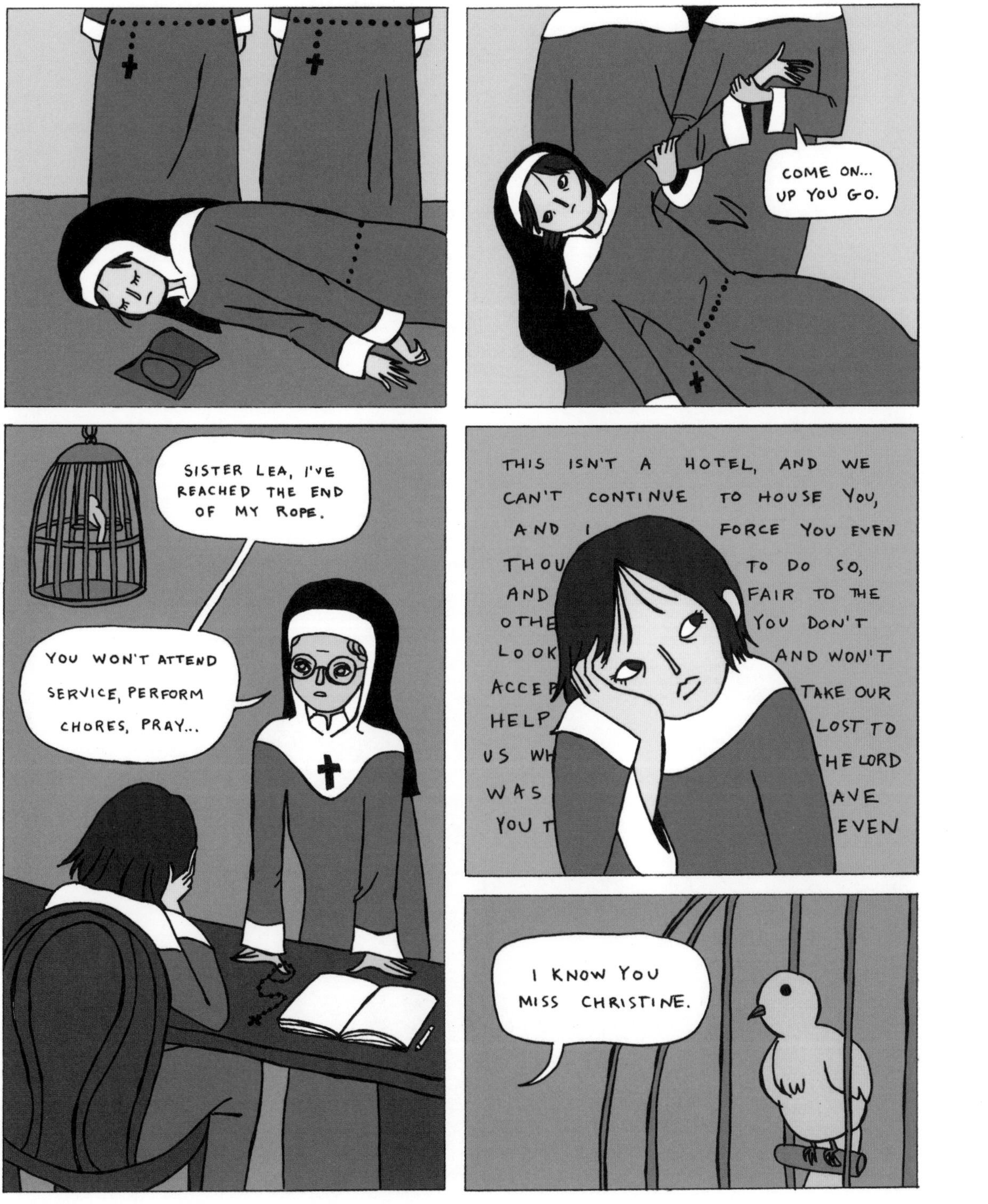
COME ON... UP YOU GO.
SISTER LEA, I'VE REACHED THE END OF MY ROPE.
YOU WON'T ATTEND SERVICE, PERFORM CHORES, PRAY...
THIS ISN'T A HOTEL, AND WE CAN'T CONTINUE TO HOUSE YOU,
AND I FORCE YOU EVEN
THOU TO DO SO,
AND FAIR TO THE
OTHE YOU DON'T
LOOK AND WON'T
ACCE TAKE OUR
HELP LOST TO
US WH THE LORD
WAS AVE
YOU T EVEN
I KNOW YOU MISS CHRISTINE.

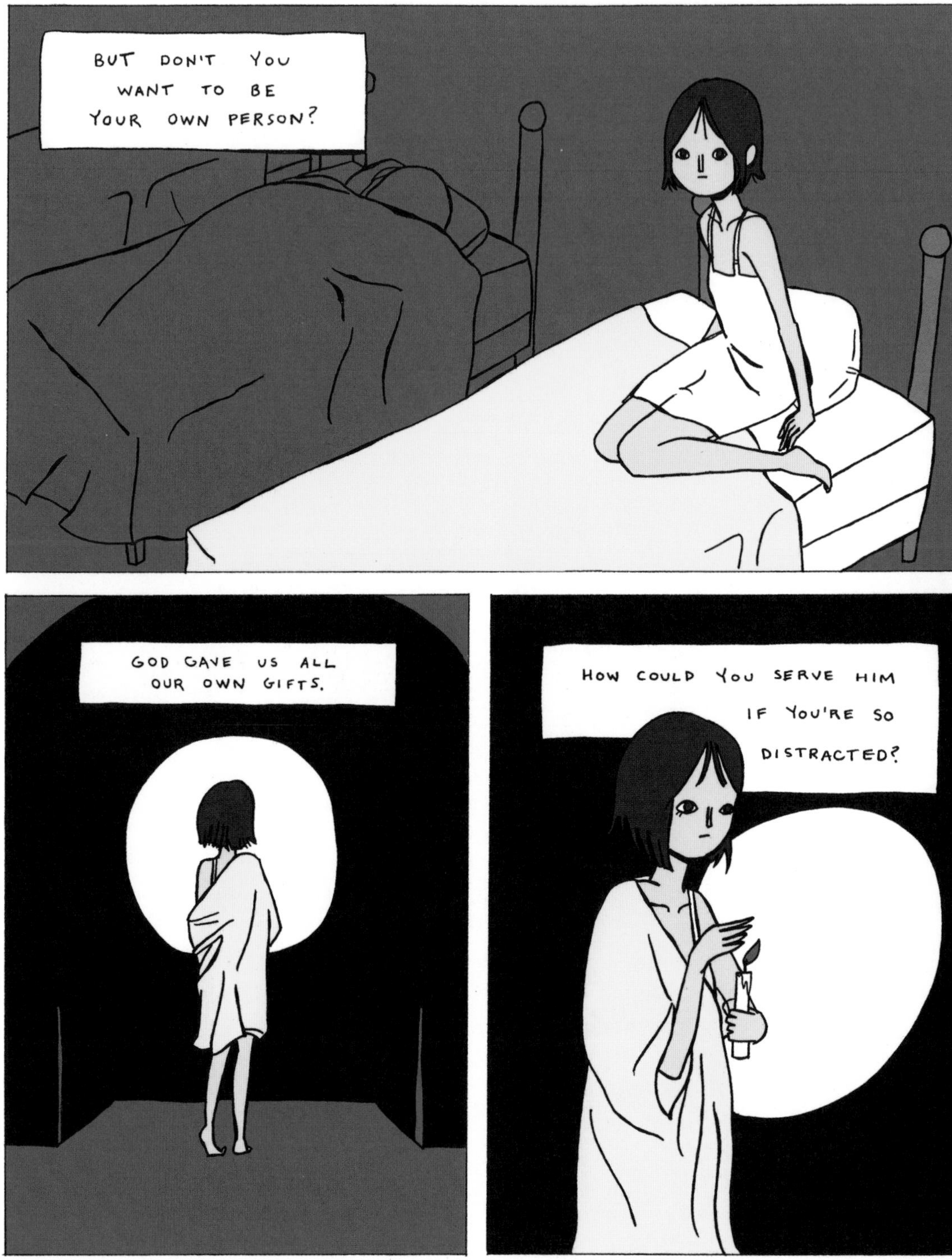
BUT DON'T YOU WANT TO BE YOUR OWN PERSON?
GOD GAVE US ALL OUR OWN GIFTS.
HOW COULD YOU SERVE HIM IF YOU'RE SO DISTRACTED?

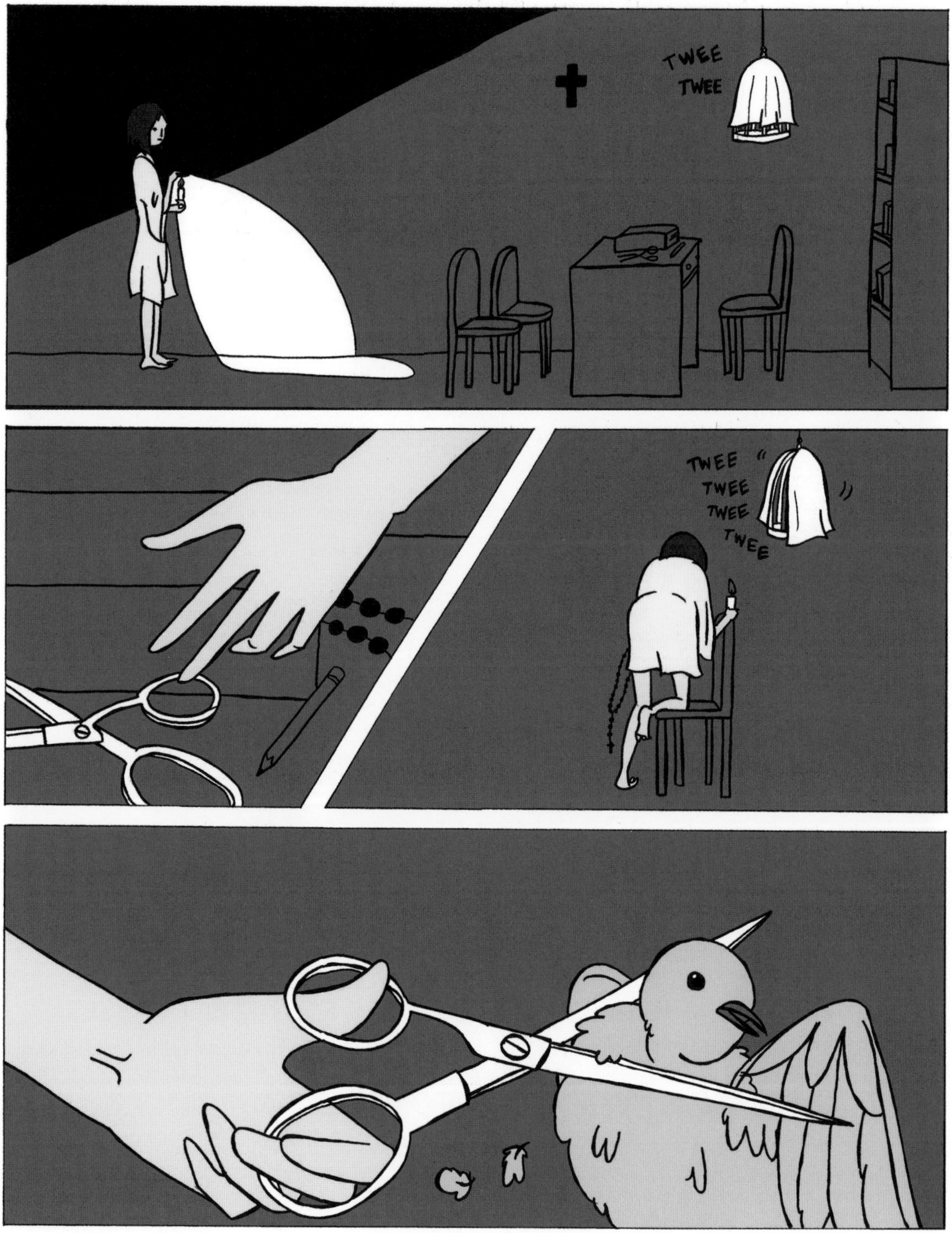
TWEE
TWEE
TWEE
TWEE
TWEE
TWEE

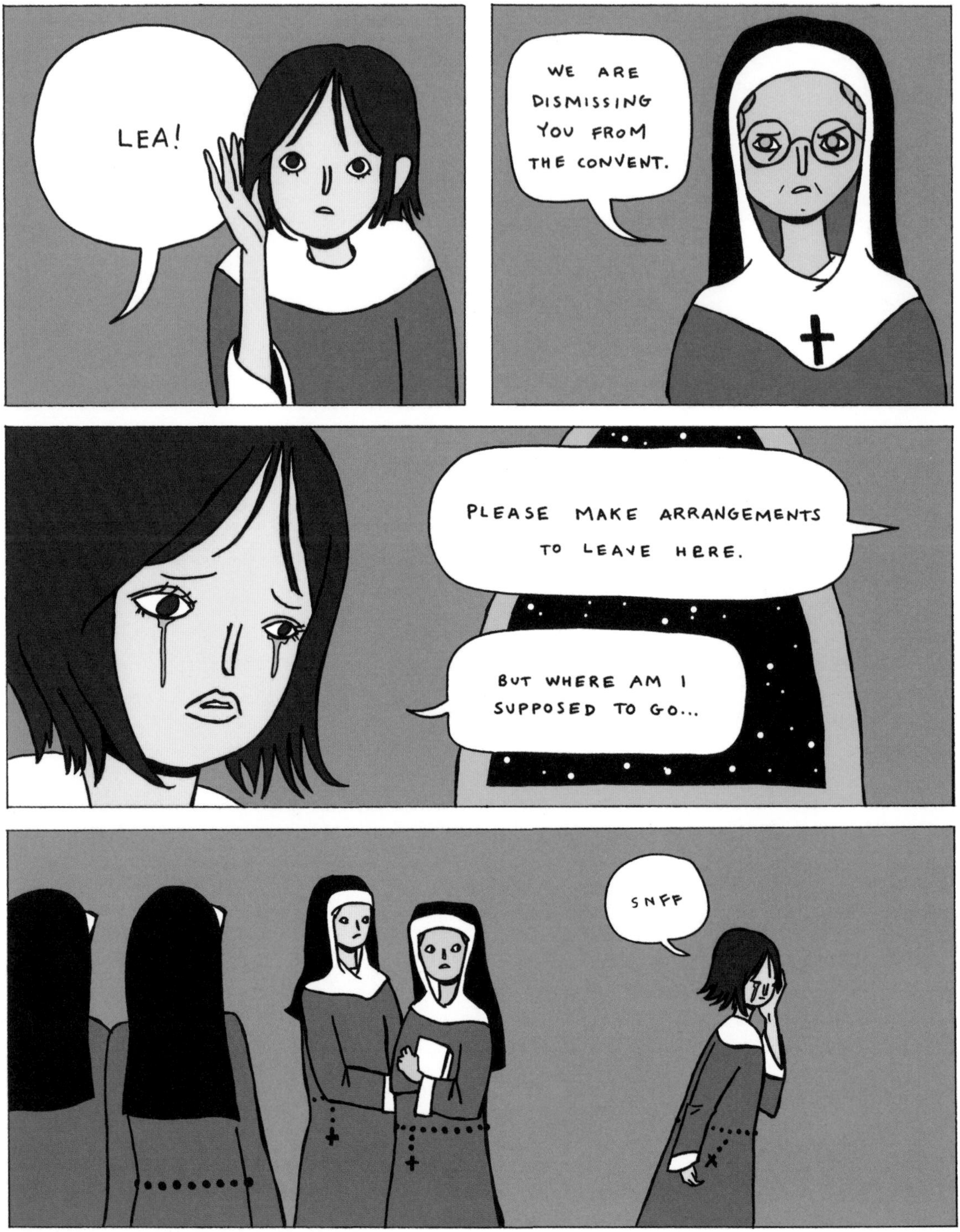
LEA!
WE ARE DISMISSING YOU FROM THE CONVENT.
PLEASE MAKE ARRANGEMENTS TO LEAVE HERE.
BUT WHERE AM I SUPPOSED TO GO...
SNFF

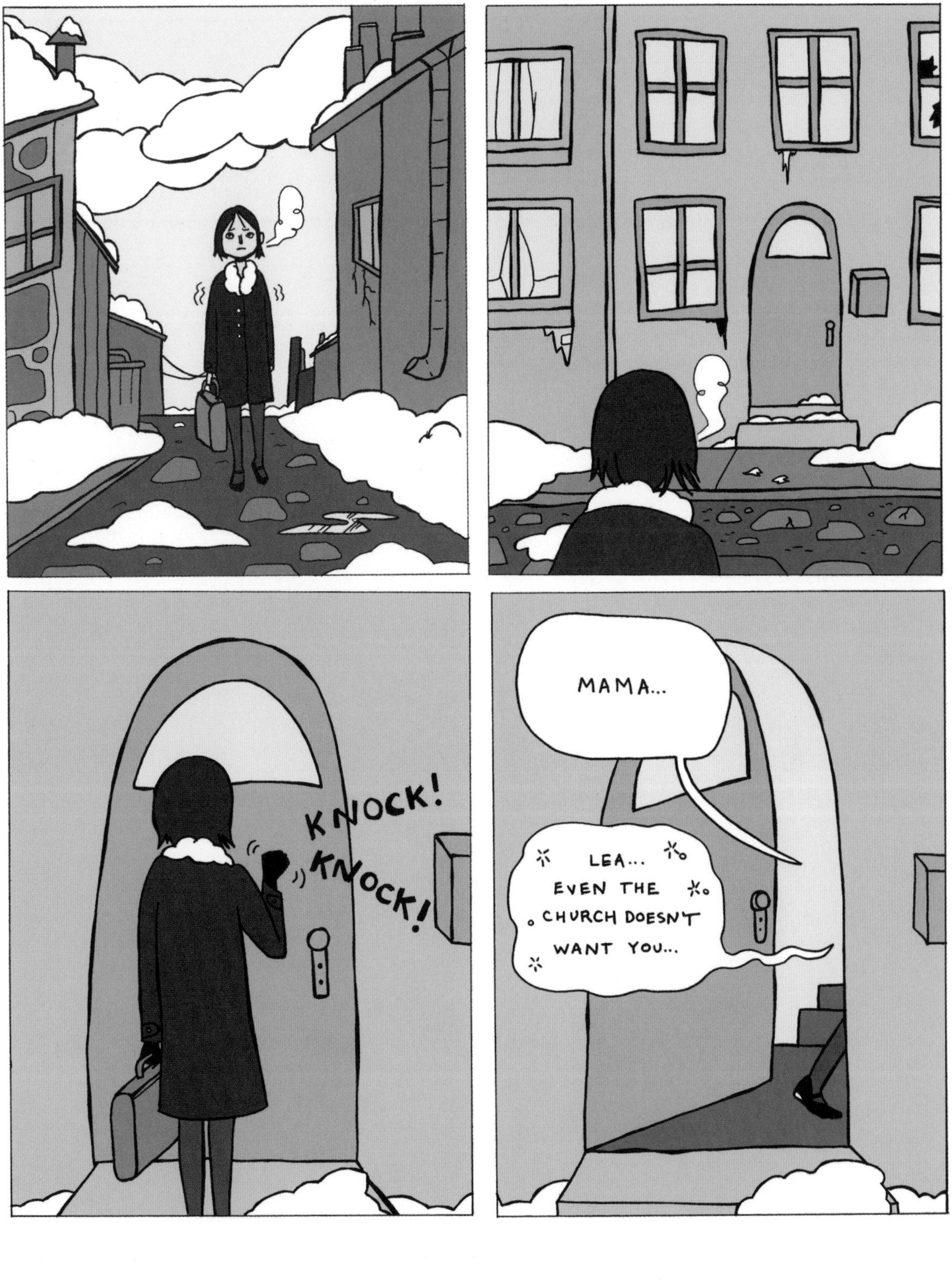
KNOCK! KNOCK!
MAMA...
LEA... EVEN THE CHURCH DOESN'T WANT YOU...

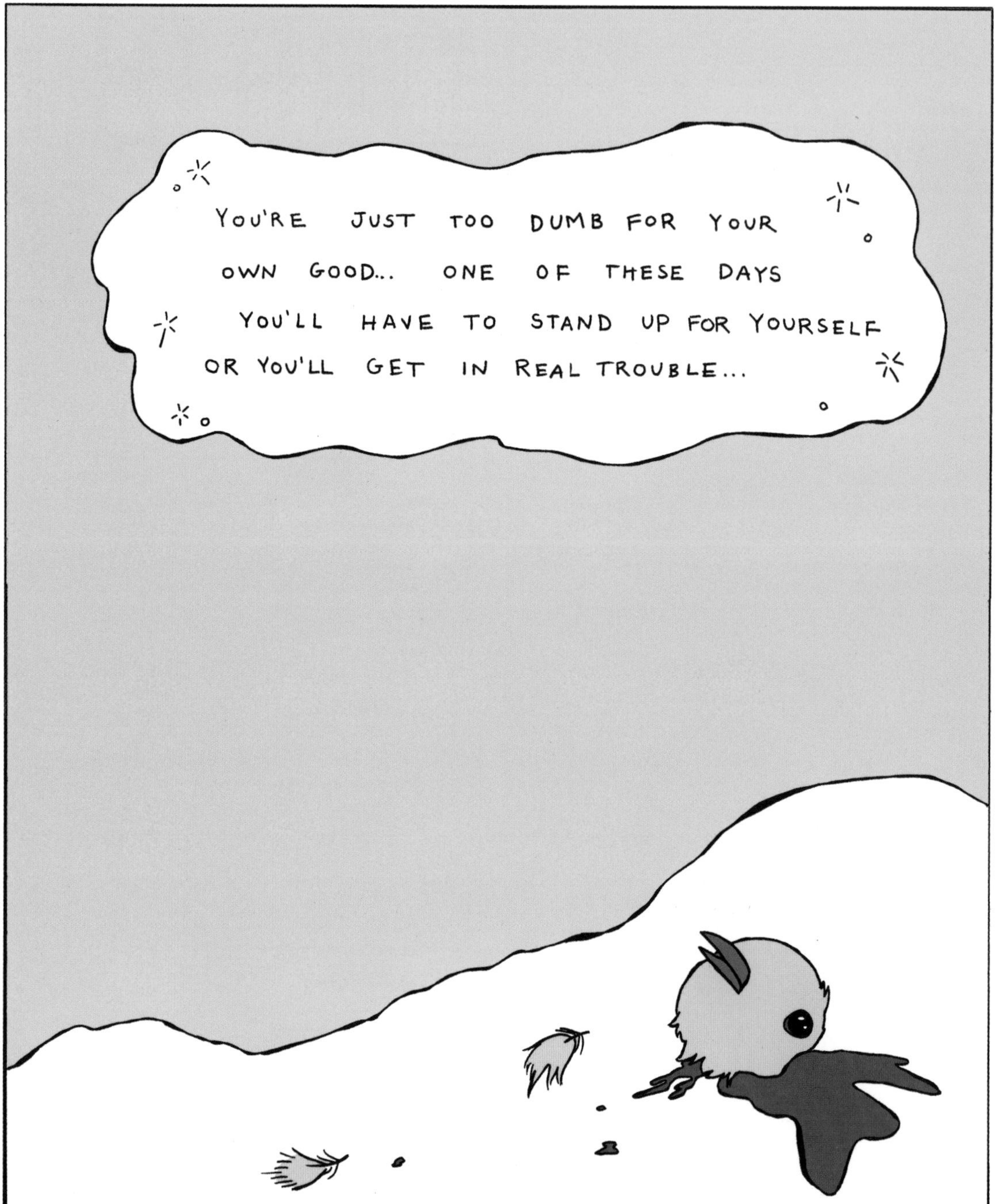
YOU'RE JUST TOO DUMB FOR YOUR OWN GOOD... ONE OF THESE DAYS YOU'LL HAVE TO STAND UP FOR YOURSELF OR YOU'LL GET IN REAL TROUBLE...

CHAPTER

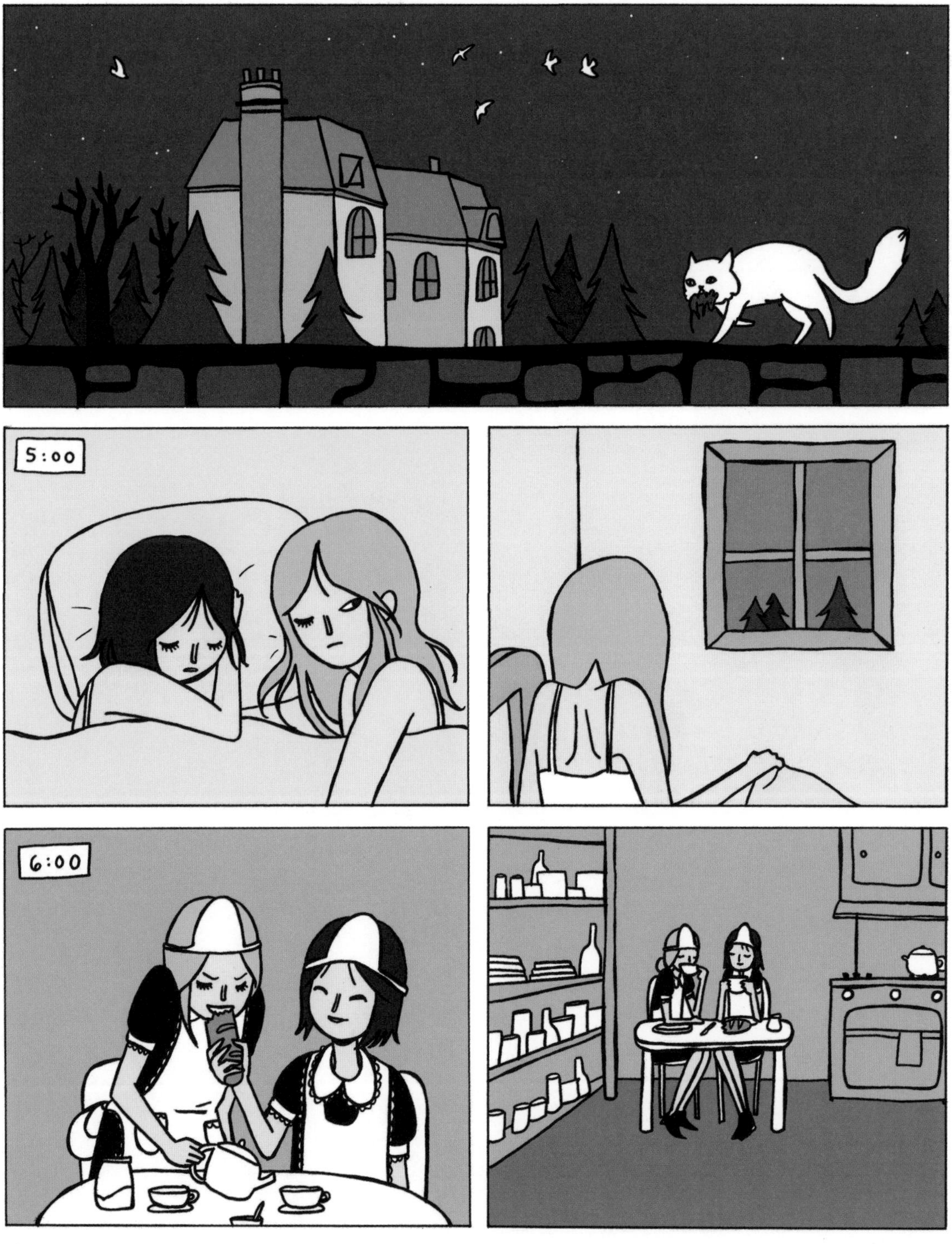
5:00
6:00

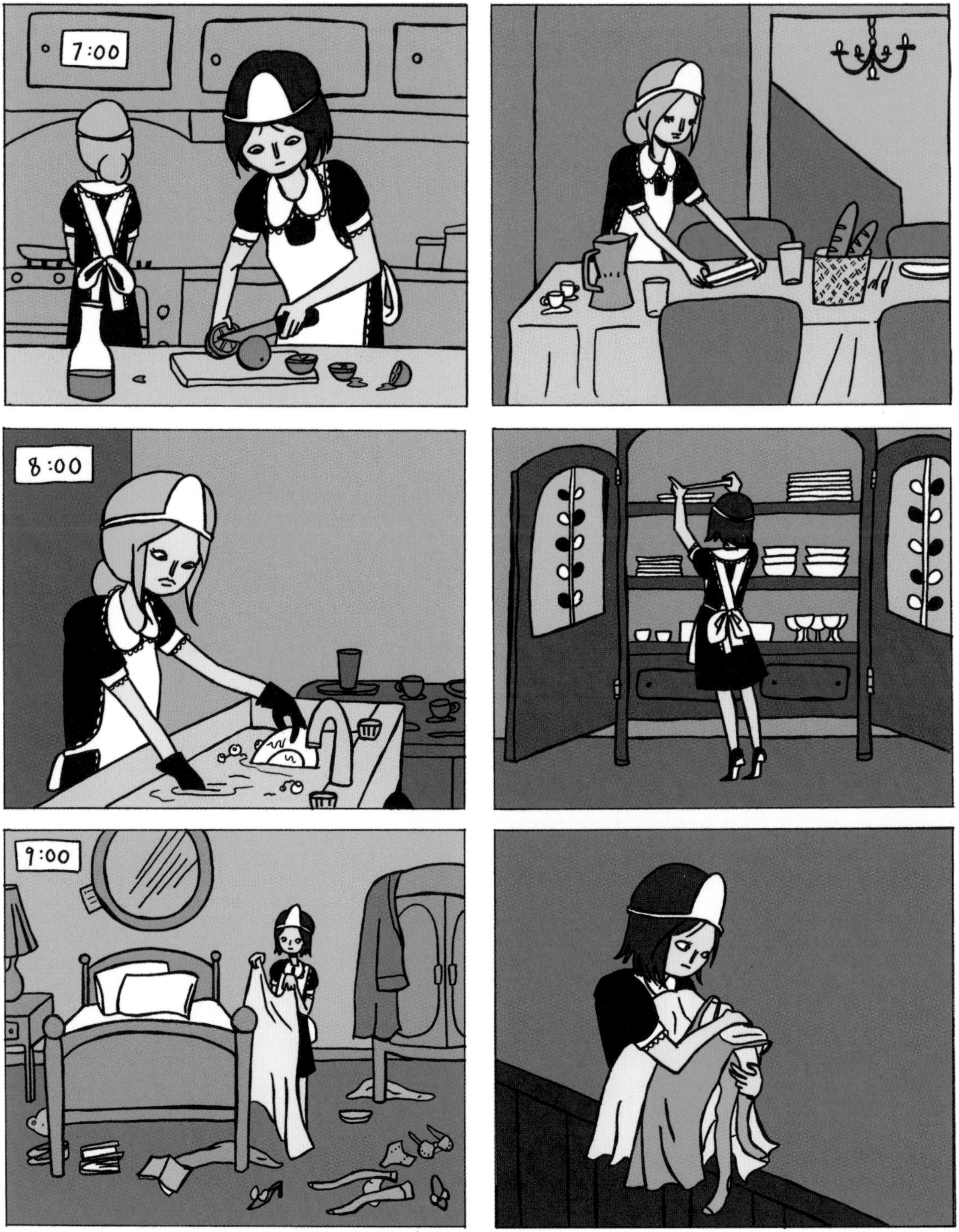
7:00
8:00
9:00

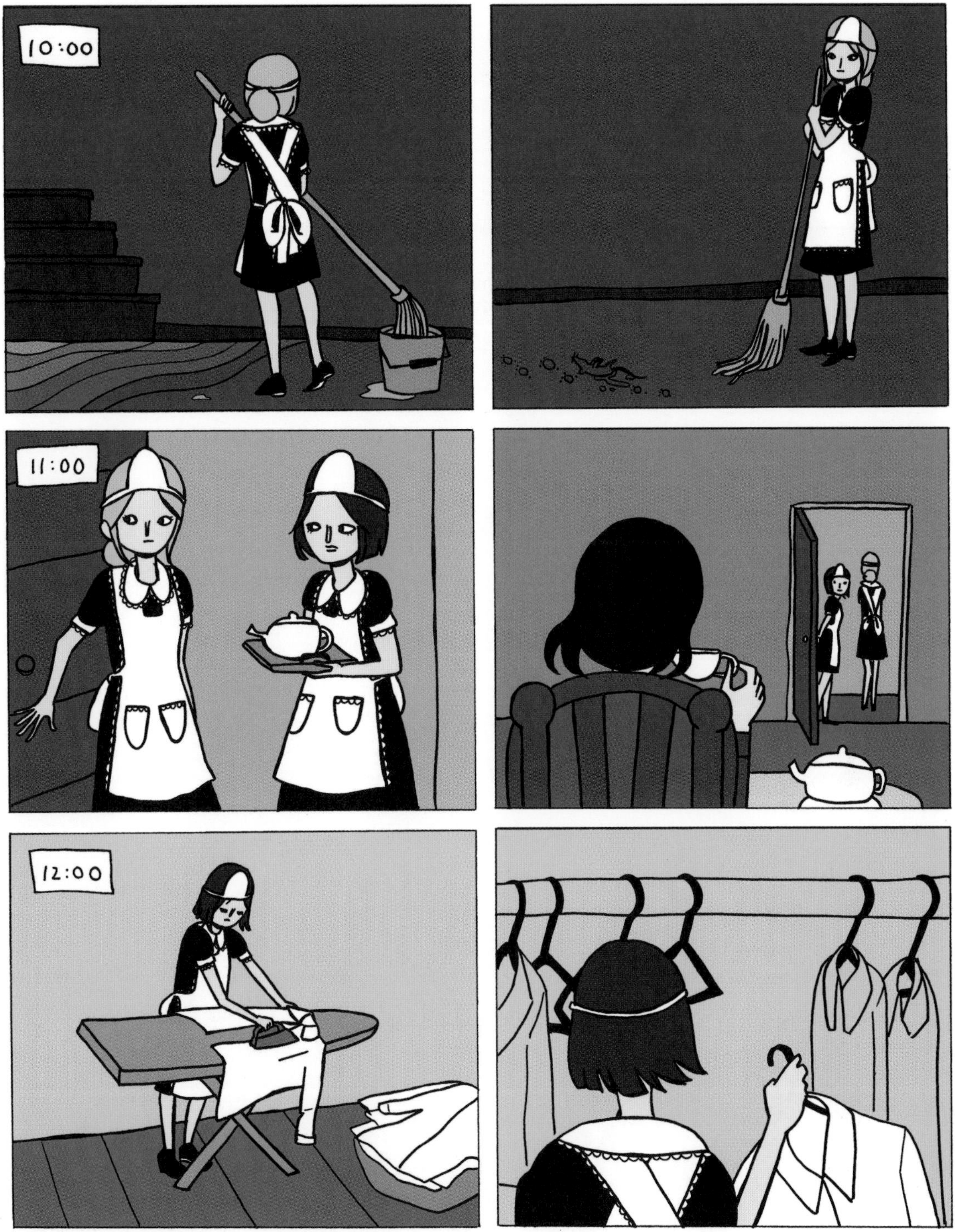
10:00
11:00
12:00

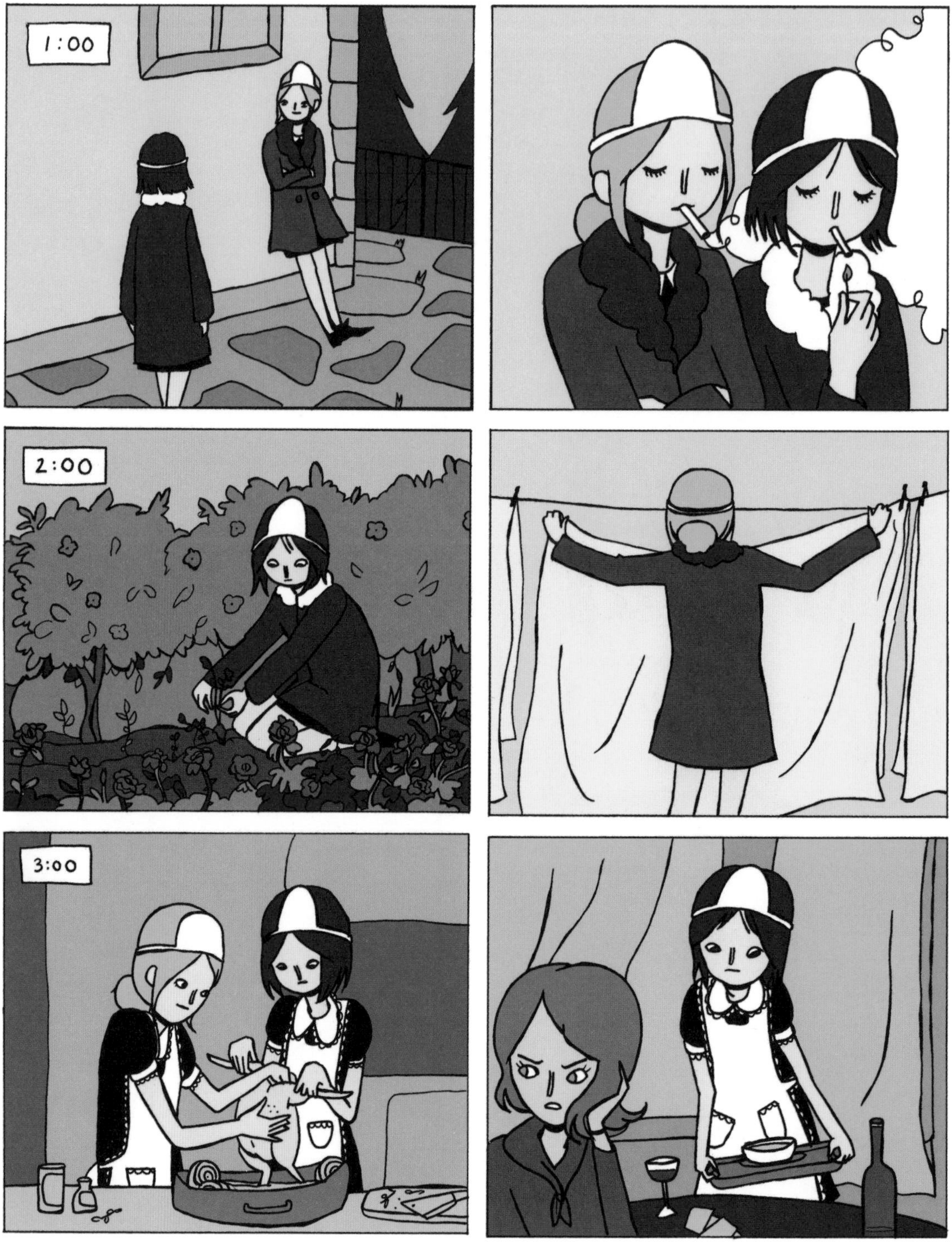
1:00
2:00
3:00

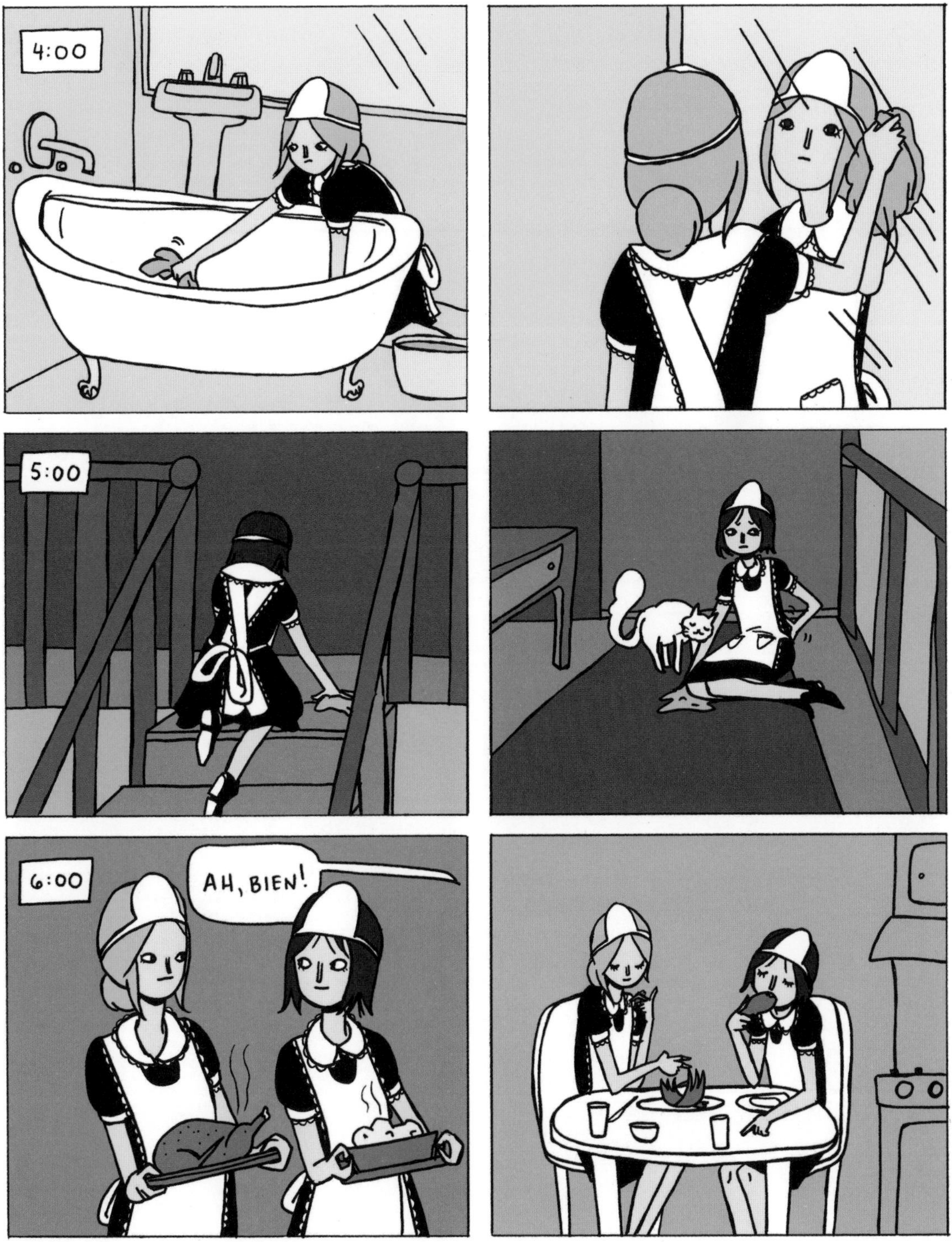
4:00
5:00
6:00
AH, BIEN!

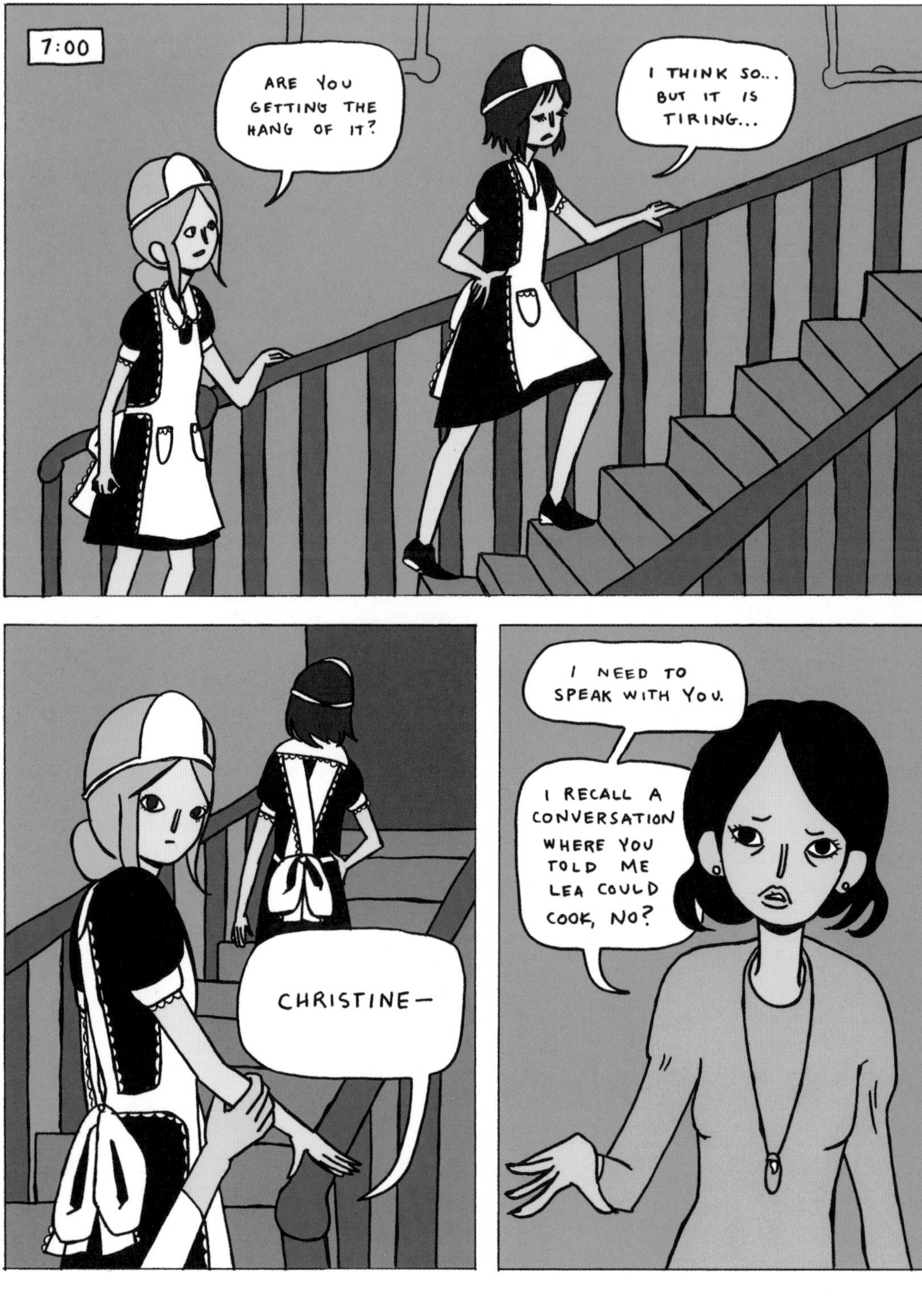
7:00
ARE YOU GETTING THE HANG OF IT?
I THINK SO... BUT IT IS TIRING...
CHRISTINE—
I NEED TO SPEAK WITH YOU.
I RECALL A CONVERSATION WHERE YOU TOLD ME LEA COULD COOK, NO?

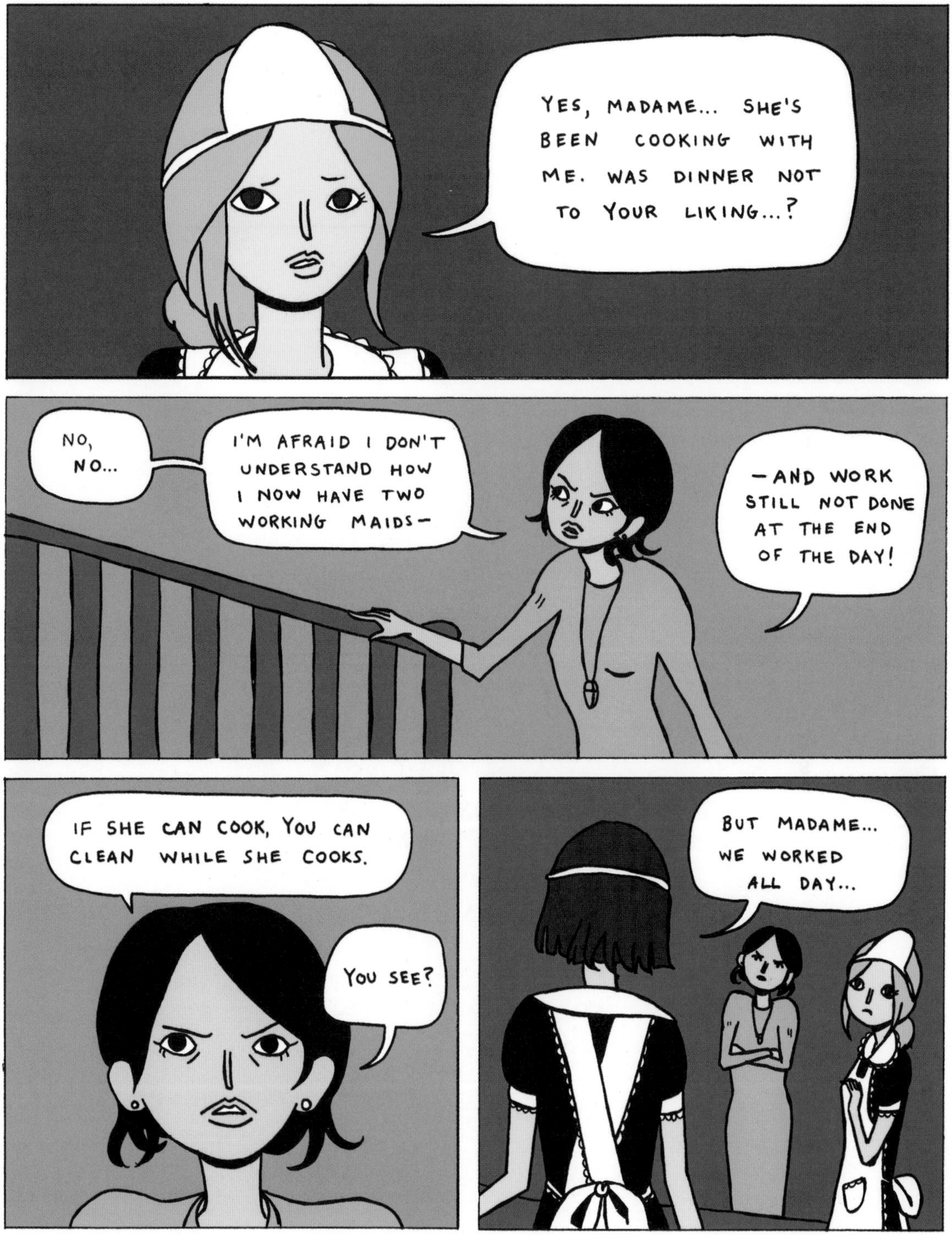
YES, MADAME... SHE'S BEEN COOKING WITH ME. WAS DINNER NOT TO YOUR LIKING...?
NO, NO...
I'M AFRAID I DON'T UNDERSTAND HOW I NOW HAVE TWO WORKING MAIDS—
—AND WORK STILL NOT DONE AT THE END OF THE DAY!
IF SHE CAN COOK, YOU CAN CLEAN WHILE SHE COOKS.
YOU SEE?
BUT MADAME... WE WORKED ALL DAY...

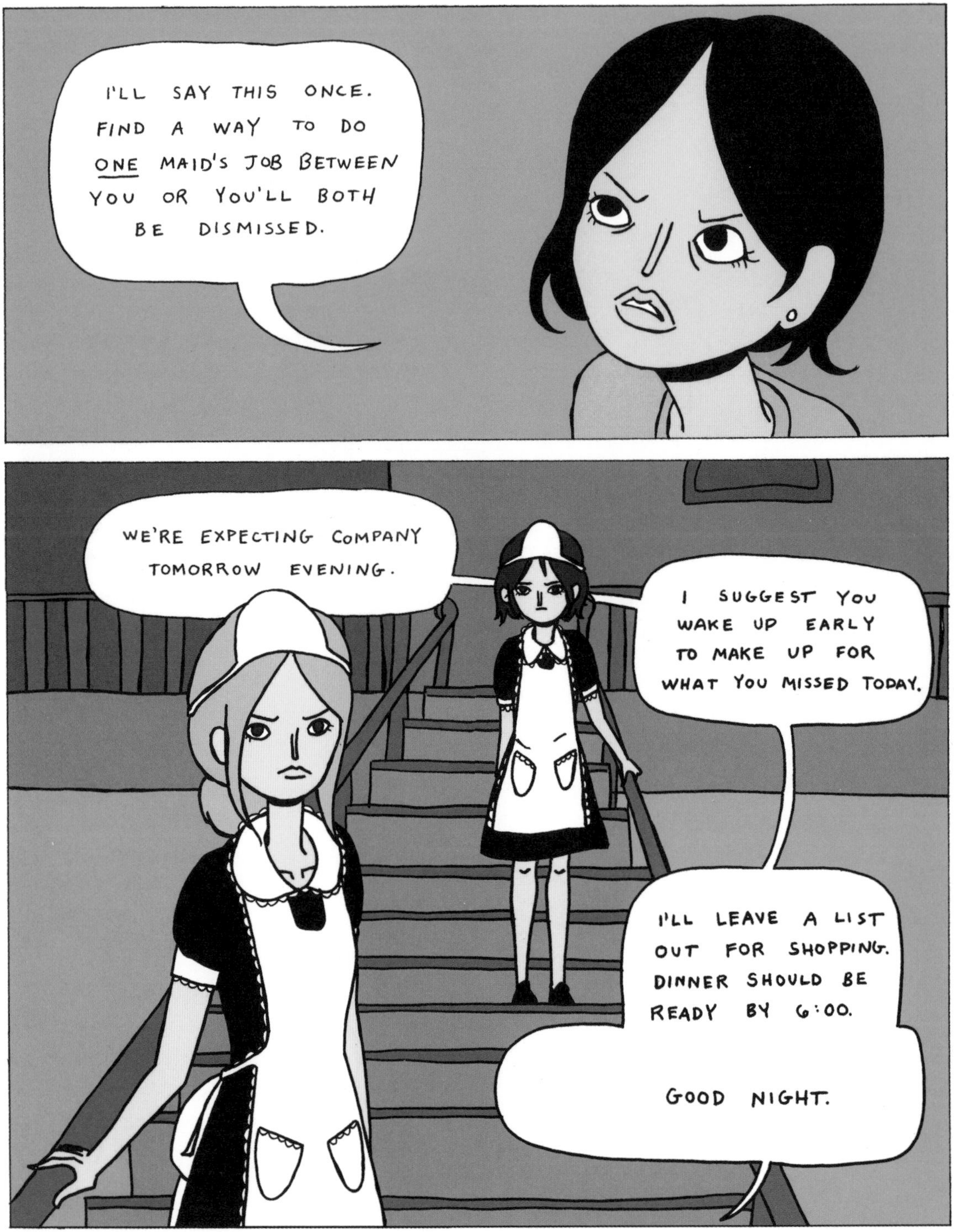
I'LL SAY THIS ONCE. FIND A WAY TO DO ONE MAID'S JOB BETWEEN YOU OR YOU'LL BOTH BE DISMISSED.
WE'RE EXPECTING COMPANY TOMORROW EVENING.
I SUGGEST YOU WAKE UP EARLY TO MAKE UP FOR WHAT YOU MISSED TODAY.
I'LL LEAVE A LIST OUT FOR SHOPPING. DINNER SHOULD BE READY BY 6:00.
GOOD NIGHT.

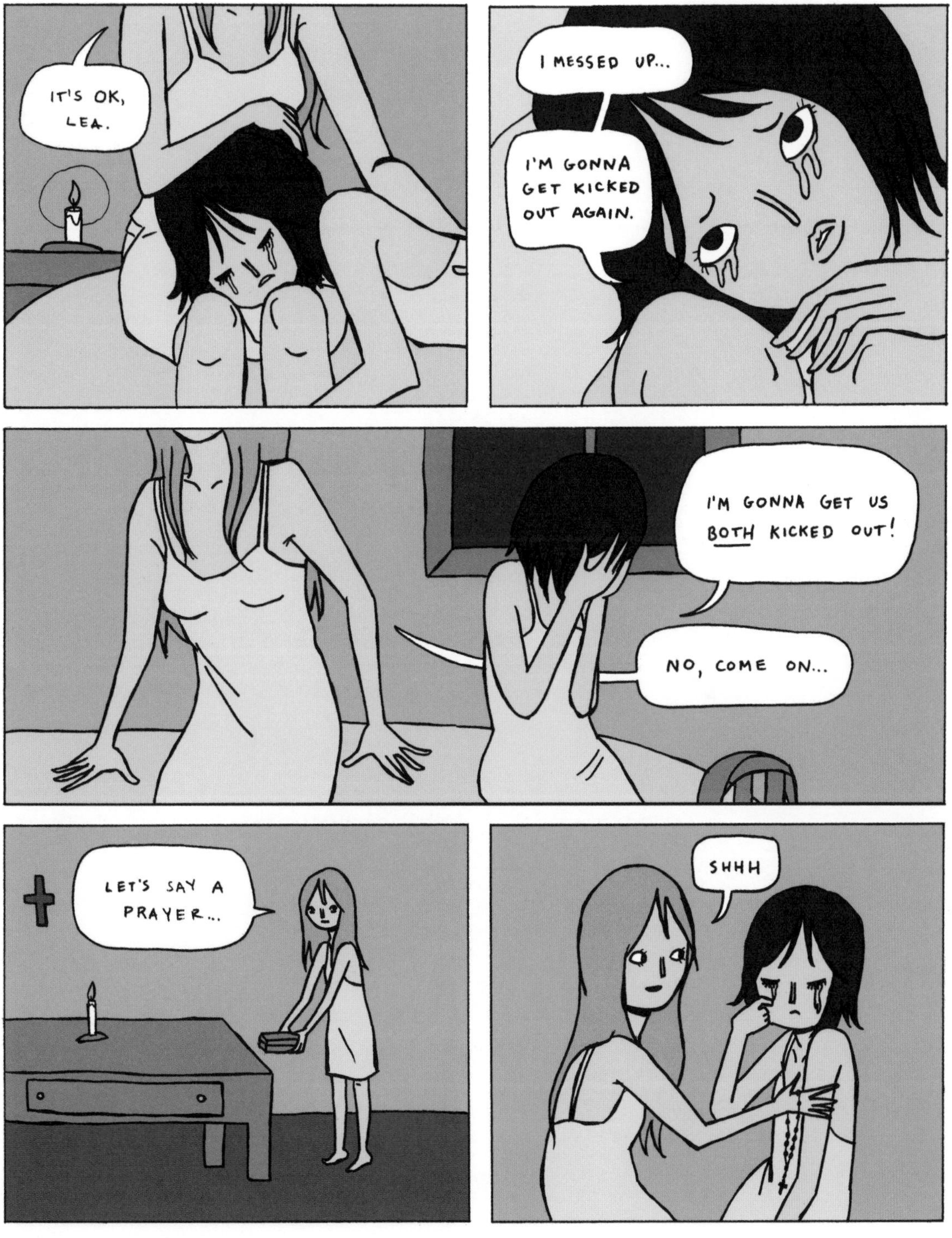
IT'S OK, LEA.
I MESSED UP...
I'M GONNA GET KICKED OUT AGAIN.
I'M GONNA GET US BOTH KICKED OUT!
NO, COME ON...
LET'S SAY A PRAYER...
SHHH

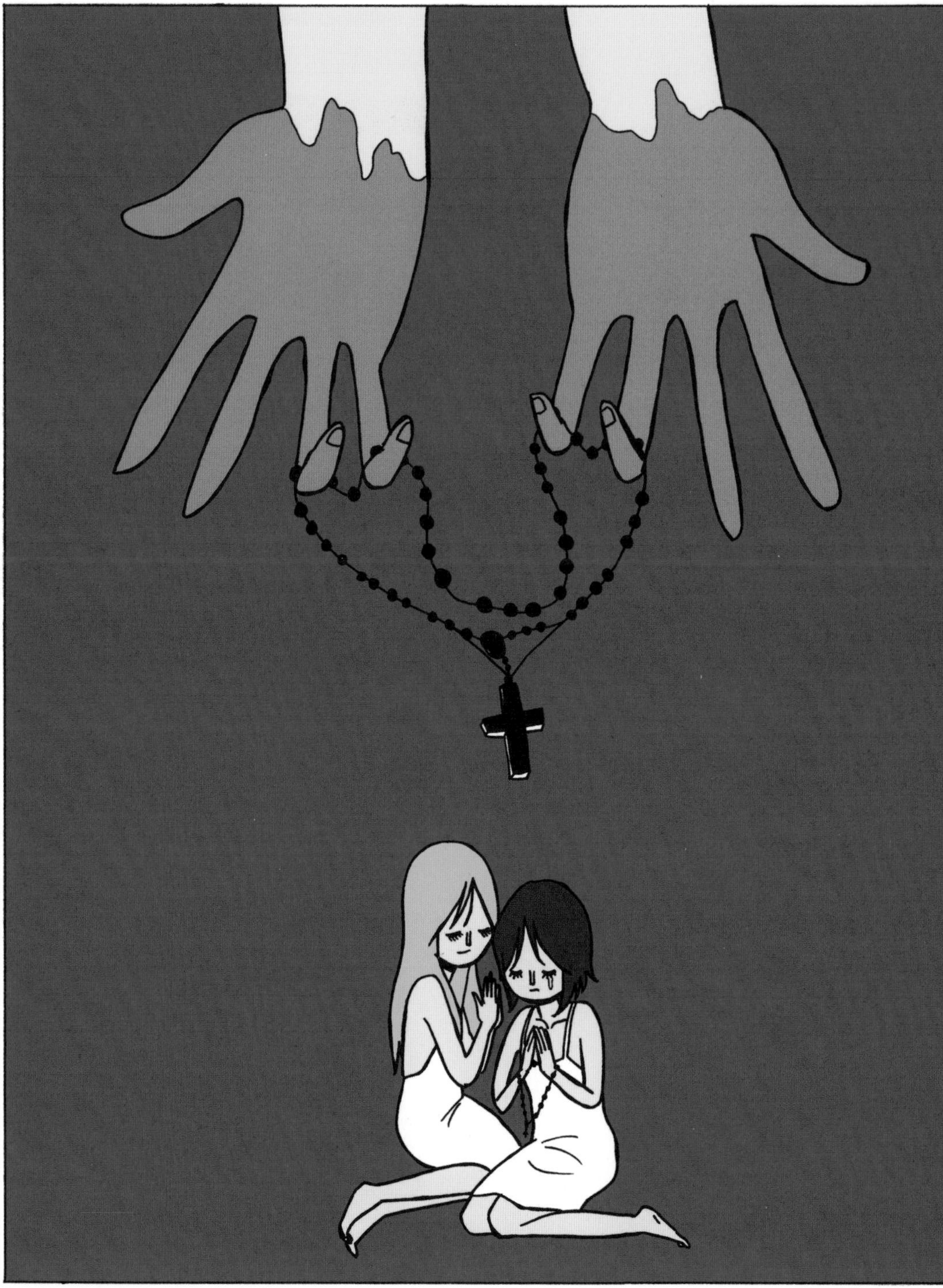

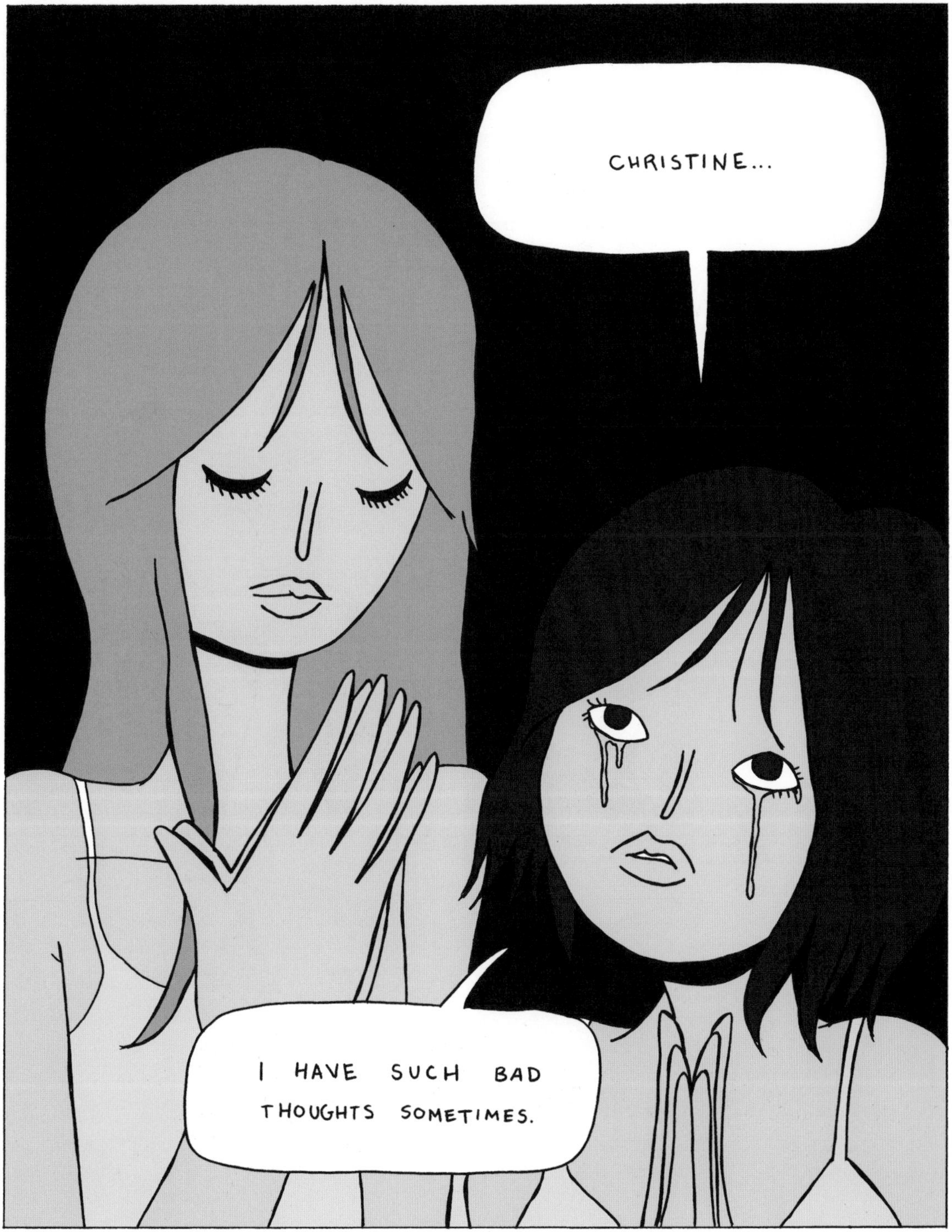
CHRISTINE...
I HAVE SUCH BAD THOUGHTS SOMETIMES.

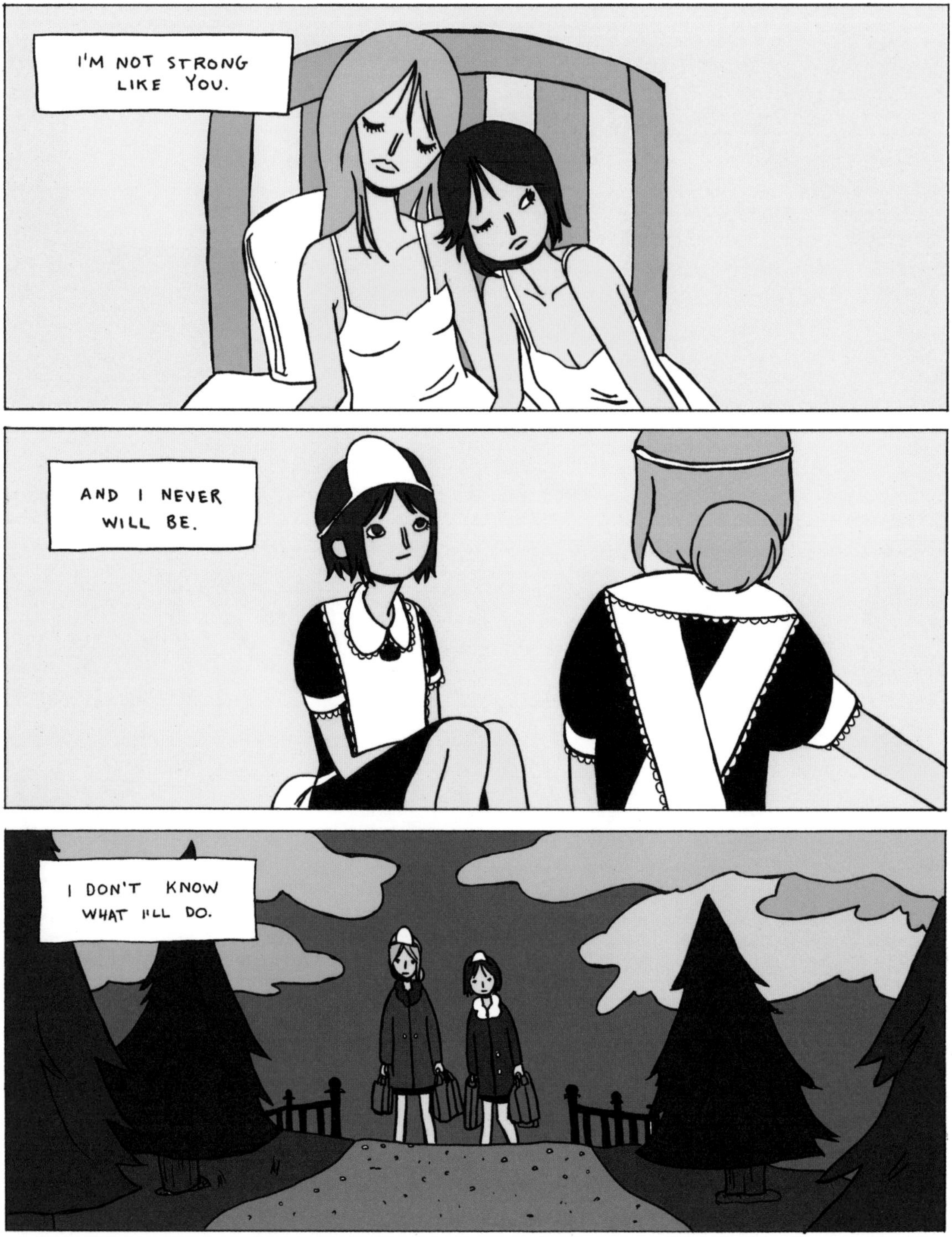
I'M NOT STRONG LIKE YOU.
AND I NEVER WILL BE.
I DON'T KNOW WHAT I'LL DO.

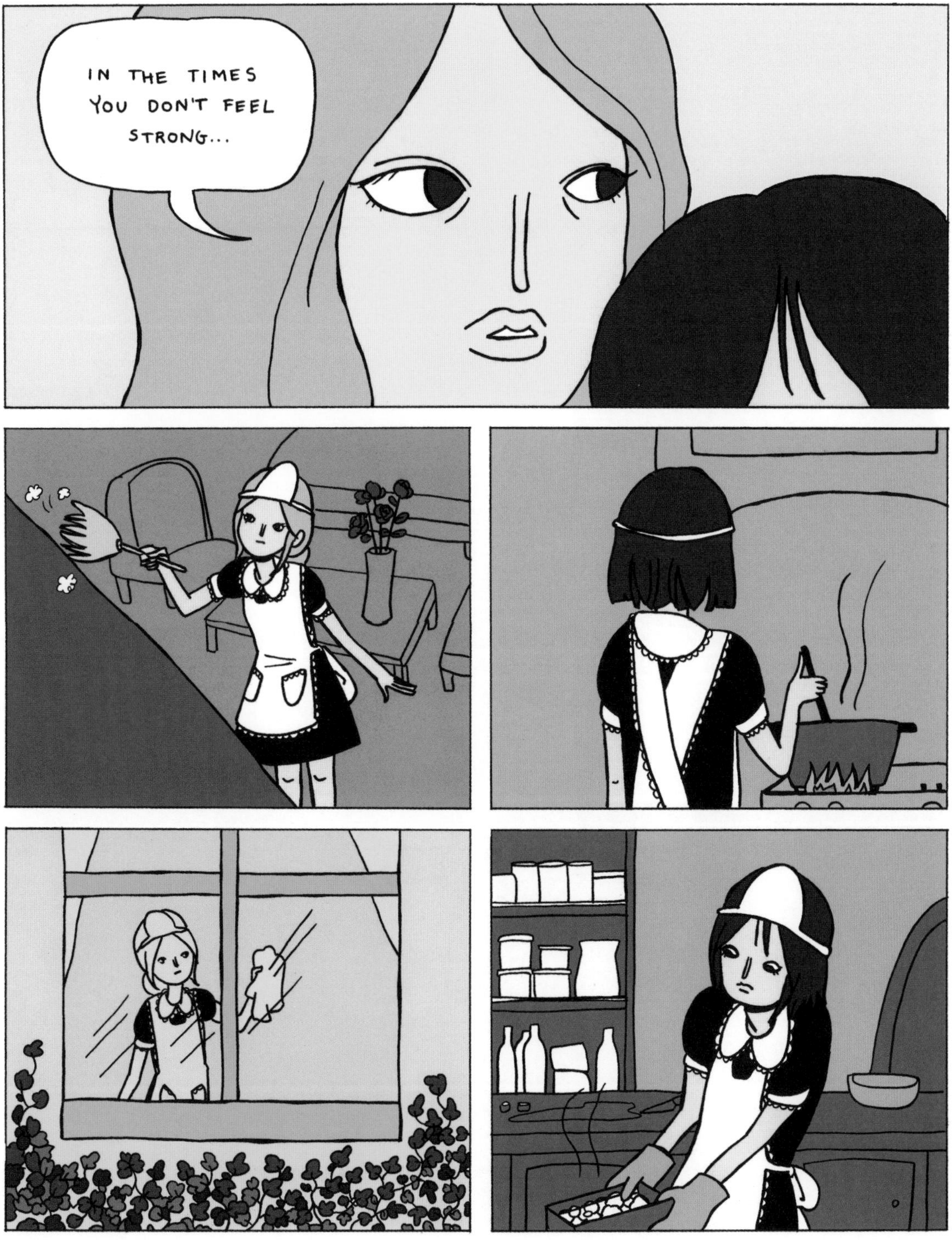
IN THE TIMES YOU DON'T FEEL STRONG...

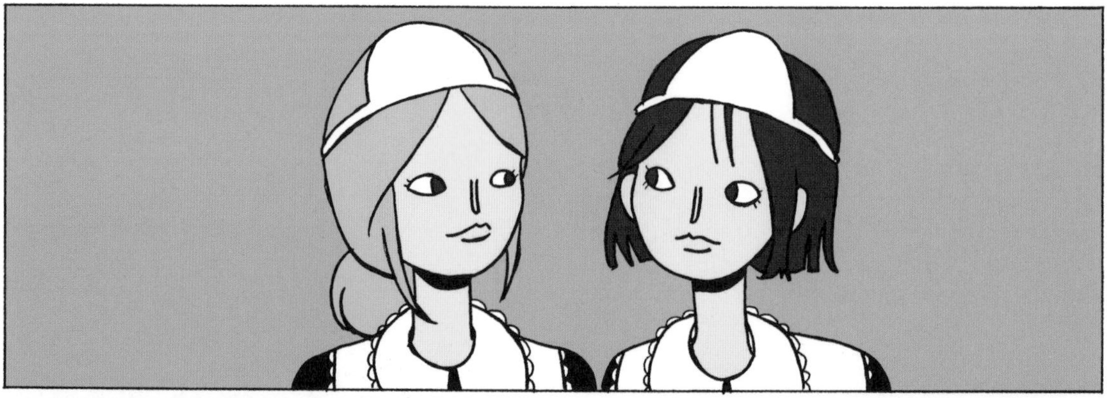

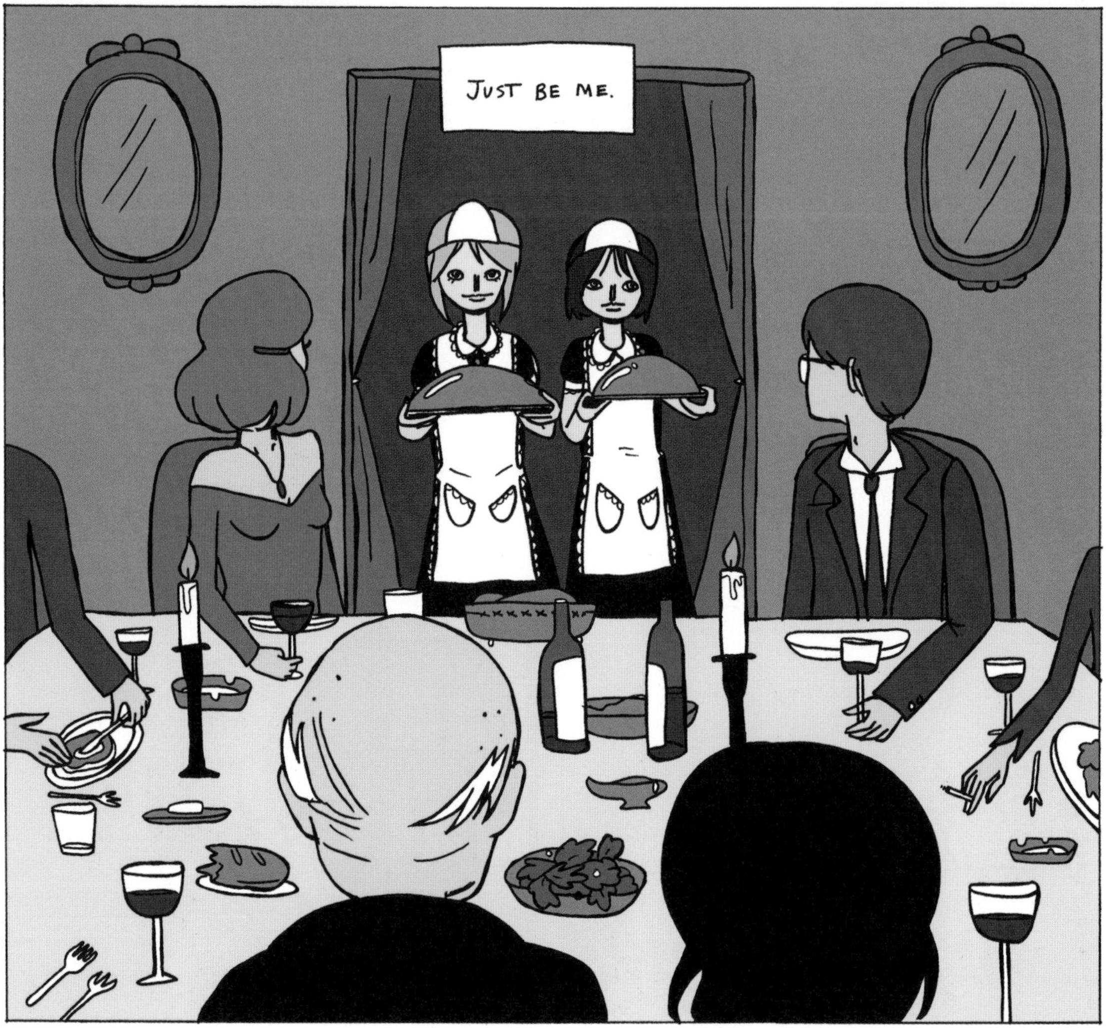
JUST BE ME.

CHAPTER

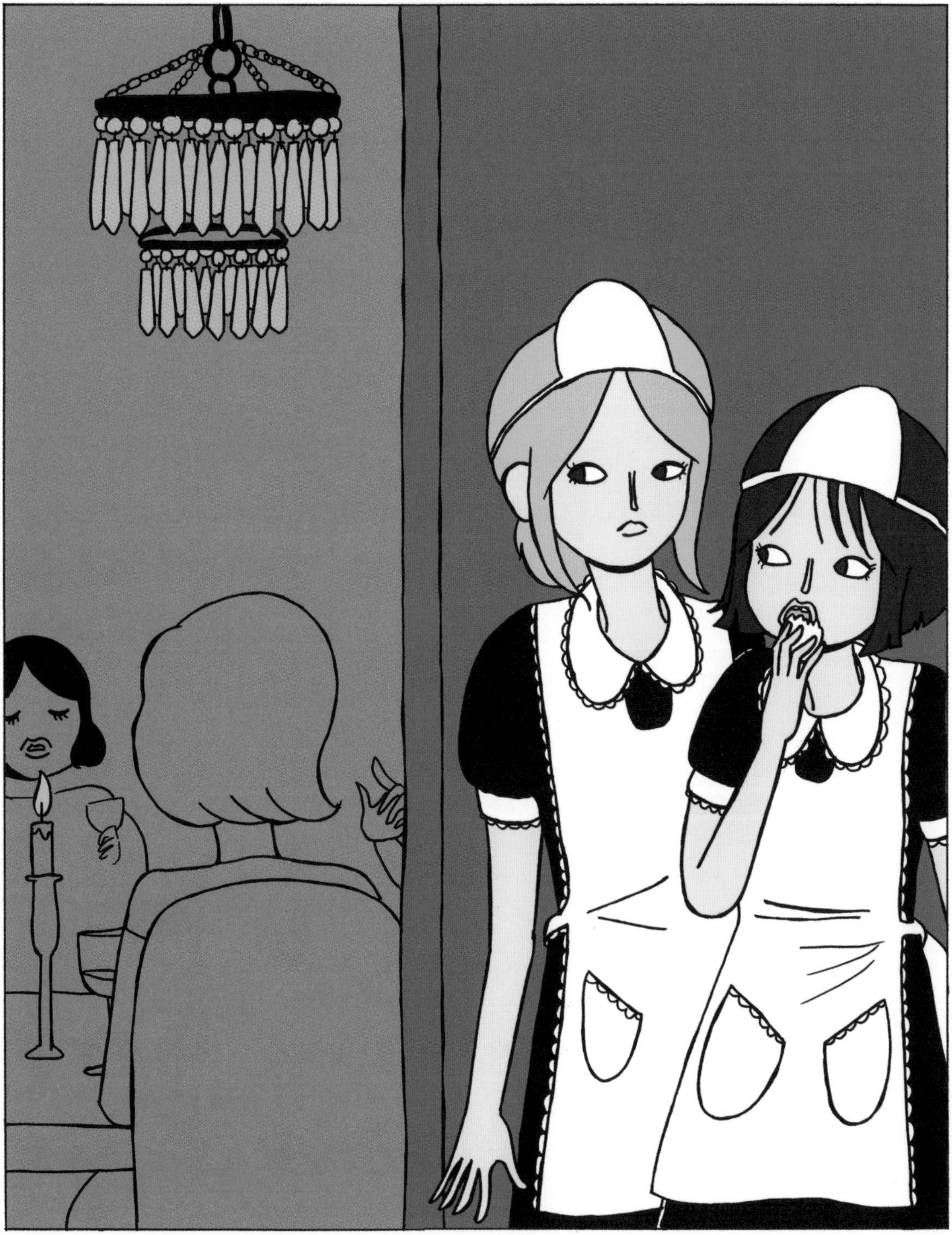

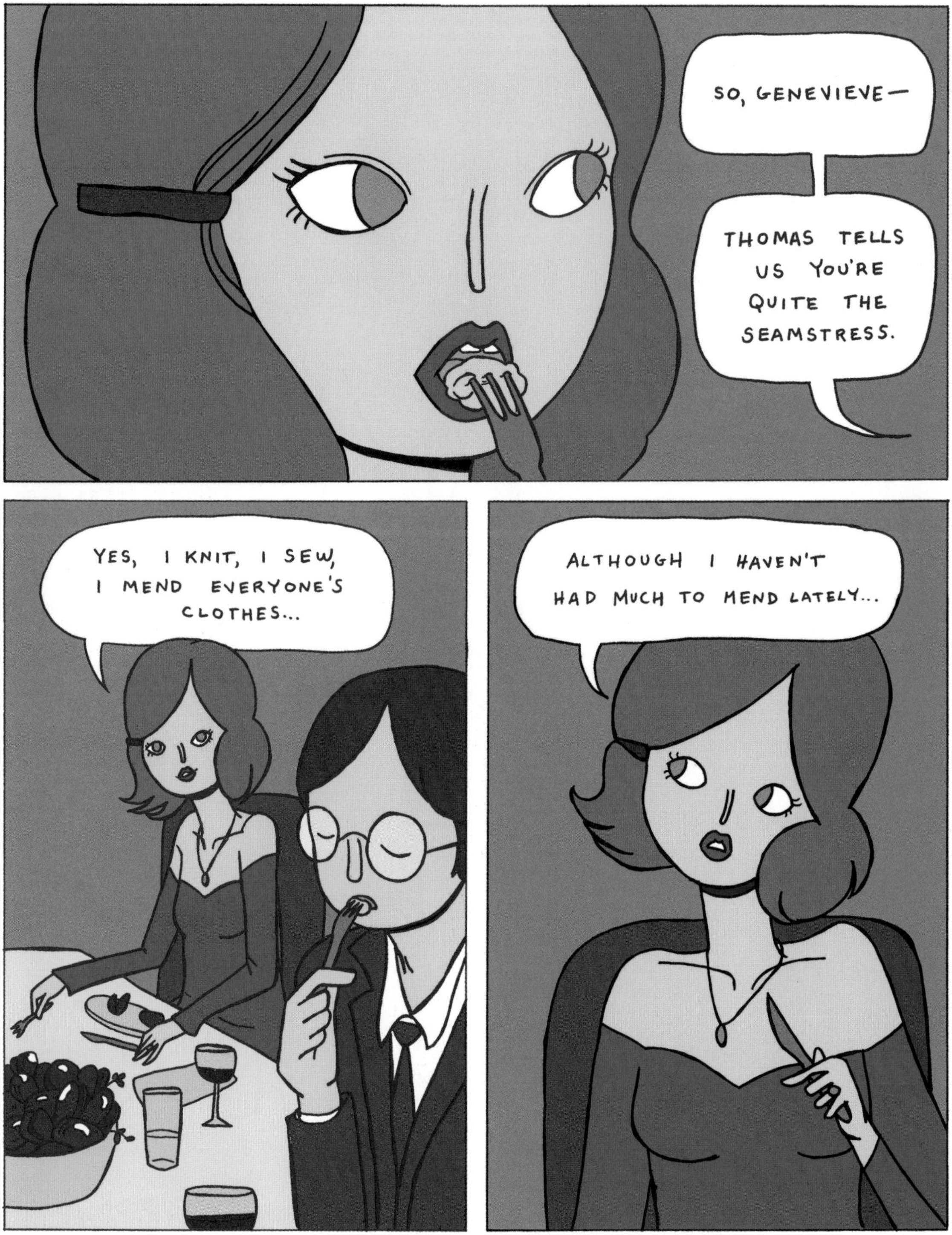
SO, GENEVIEVE—
THOMAS TELLS US YOU'RE QUITE THE SEAMSTRESS.
YES, I KNIT, I SEW, I MEND EVERYONE'S CLOTHES...
ALTHOUGH I HAVEN'T HAD MUCH TO MEND LATELY...

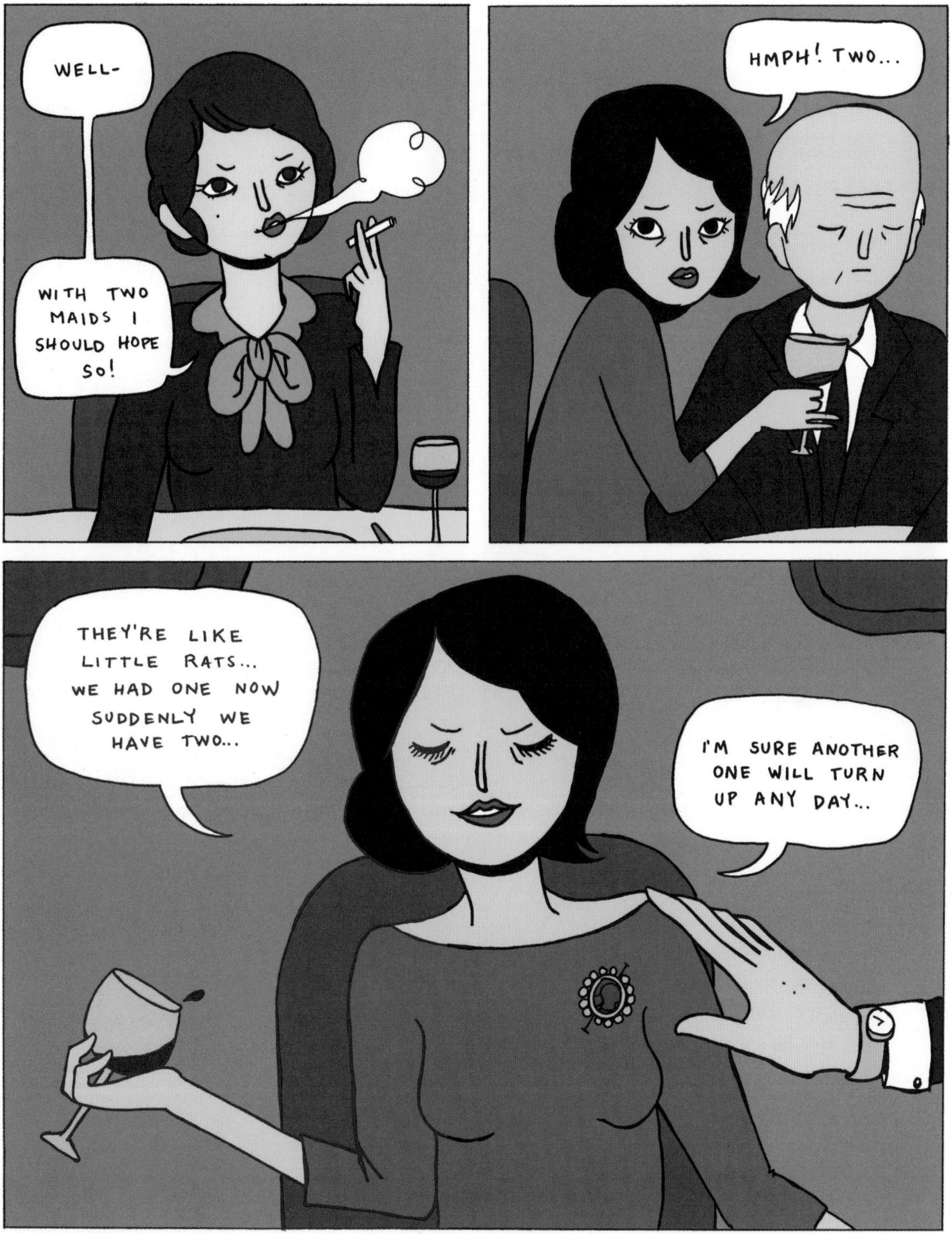
WELL-
WITH TWO MAIDS I SHOULD HOPE SO!
HMPH! TWO...
THEY'RE LIKE LITTLE RATS... WE HAD ONE NOW SUDDENLY WE HAVE TWO...
I'M SURE ANOTHER ONE WILL TURN UP ANY DAY...

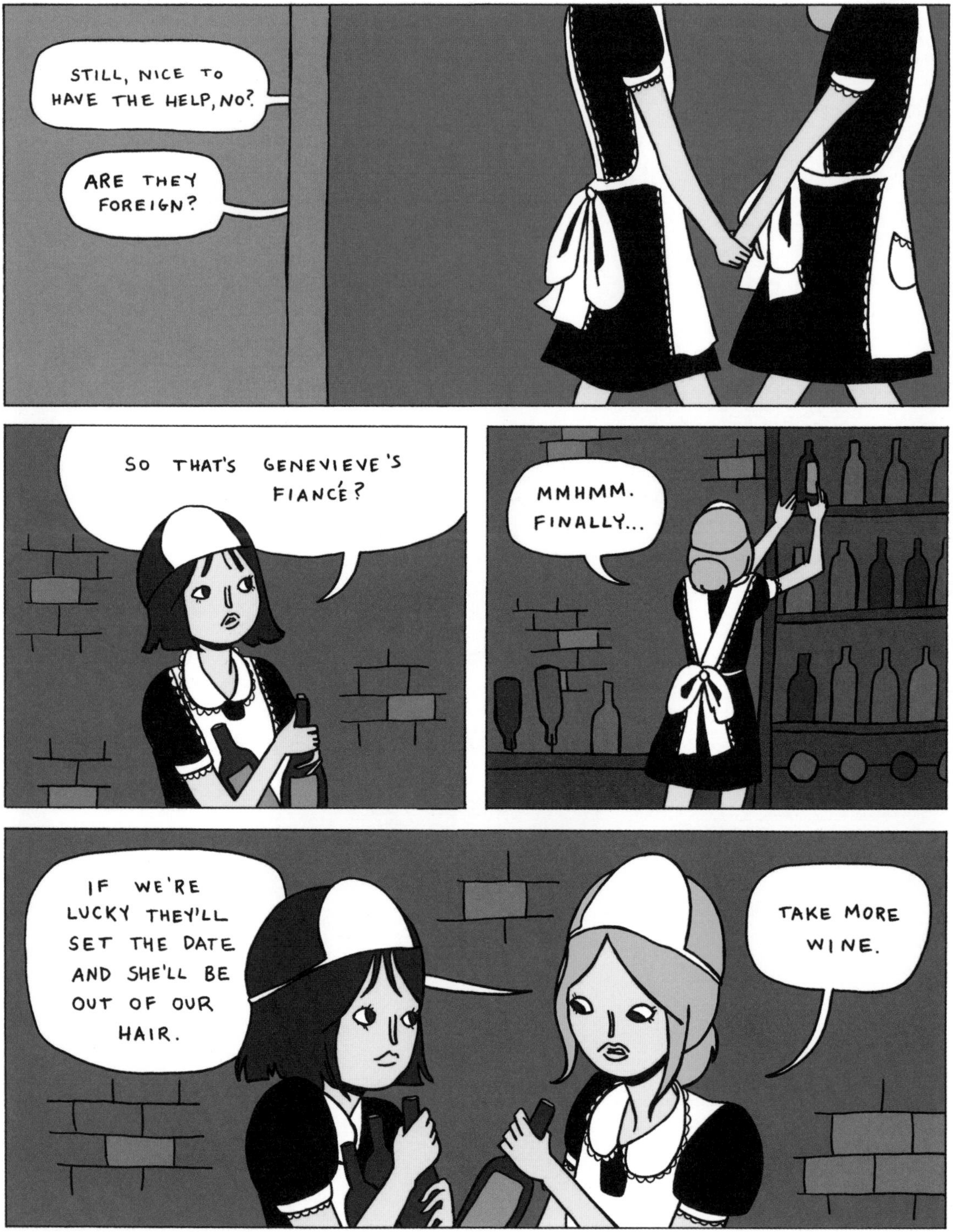
STILL, NICE TO HAVE THE HELP, NO?
ARE THEY FOREIGN?
SO THAT'S GENEVIEVE'S FIANCÉ?
MMHMM. FINALLY...
IF WE'RE LUCKY THEY'LL SET THE DATE AND SHE'LL BE OUT OF OUR HAIR.
TAKE MORE WINE.

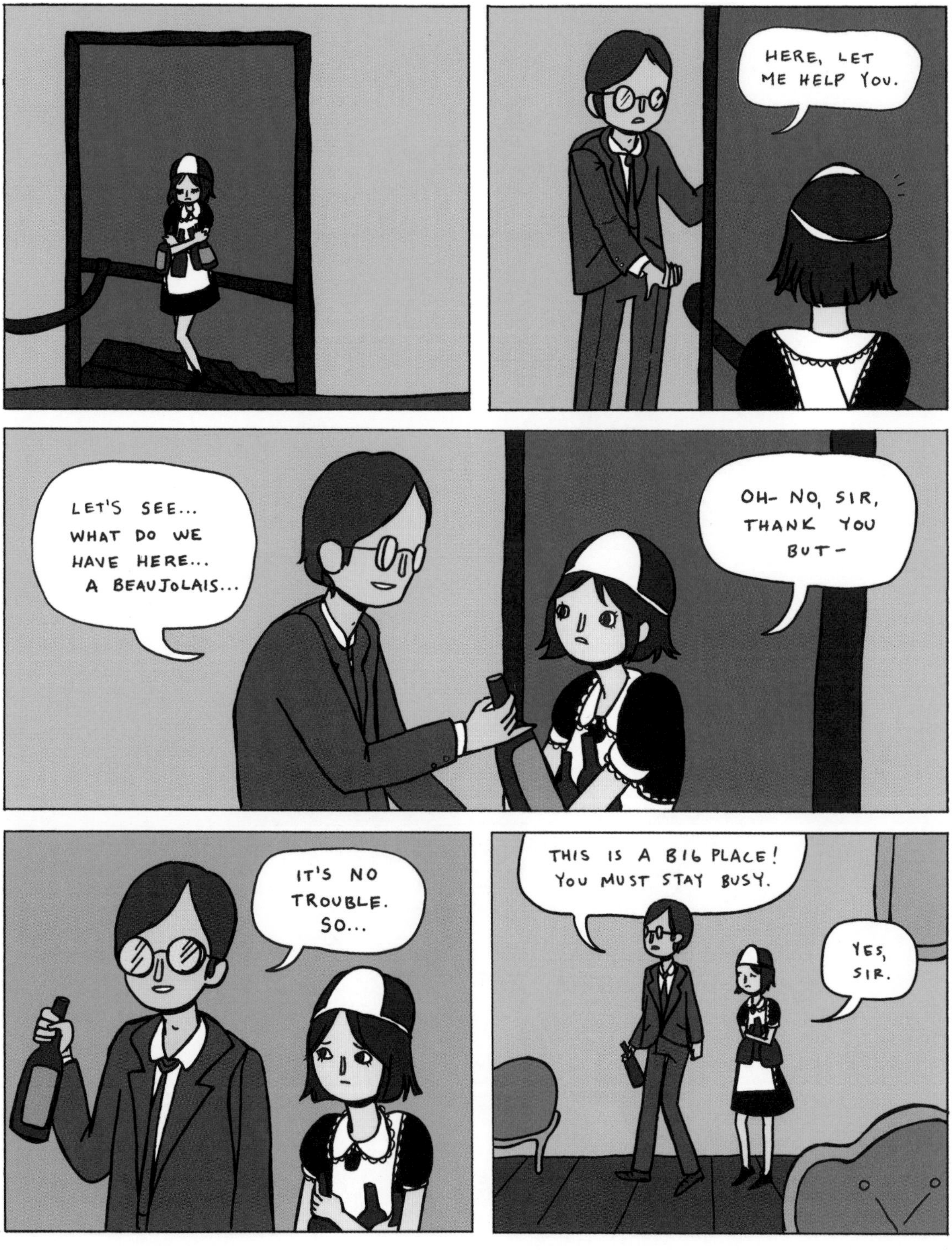
HERE, LET ME HELP YOU.
LET'S SEE... WHAT DO WE HAVE HERE... A BEAUJOLAIS...
OH- NO, SIR, THANK YOU BUT-
IT'S NO TROUBLE. SO...
THIS IS A BIG PLACE! YOU MUST STAY BUSY.
YES, SIR.

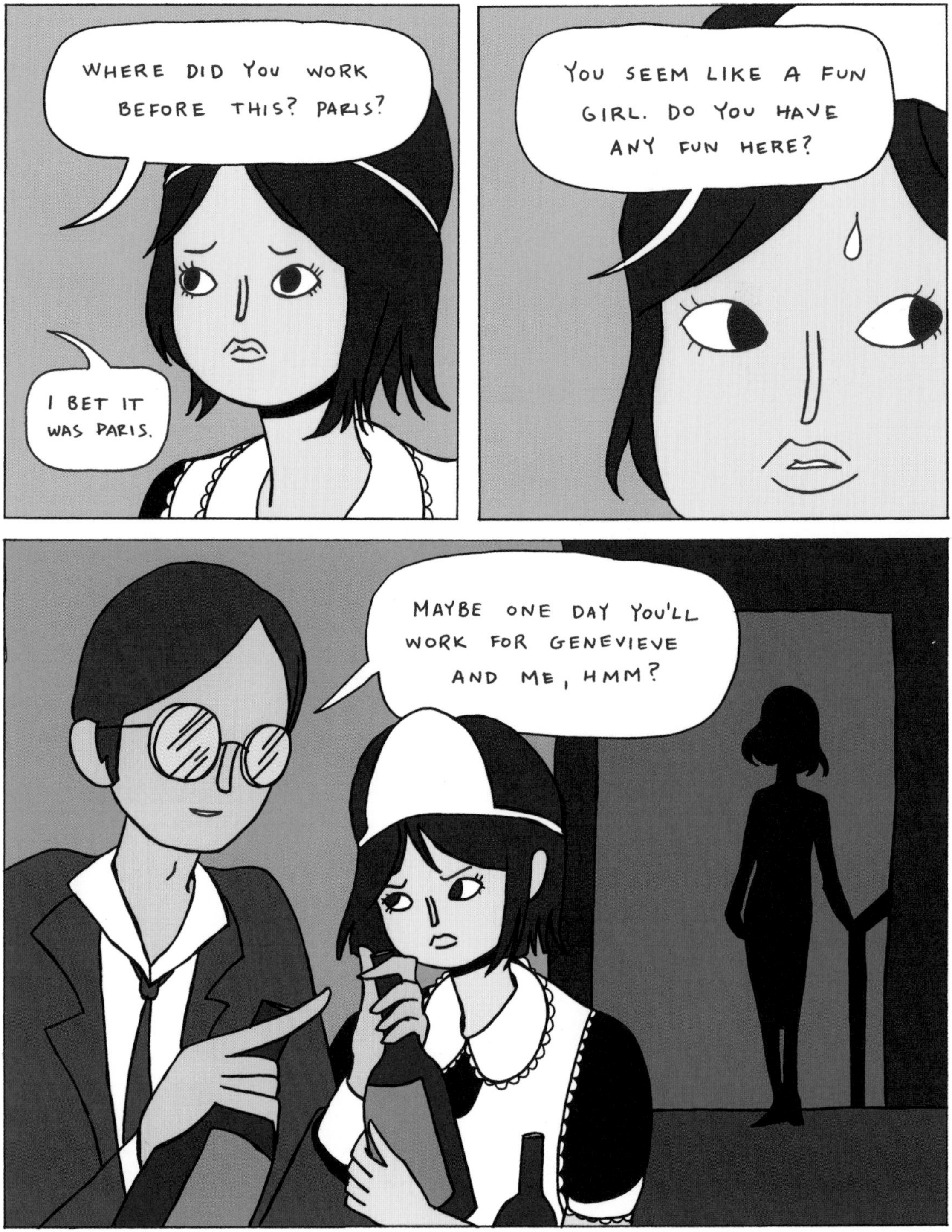
WHERE DID YOU WORK BEFORE THIS? PARIS?
I BET IT WAS PARIS.
YOU SEEM LIKE A FUN GIRL. DO YOU HAVE ANY FUN HERE?
MAYBE ONE DAY YOU'LL WORK FOR GENEVIEVE AND ME, HMM?

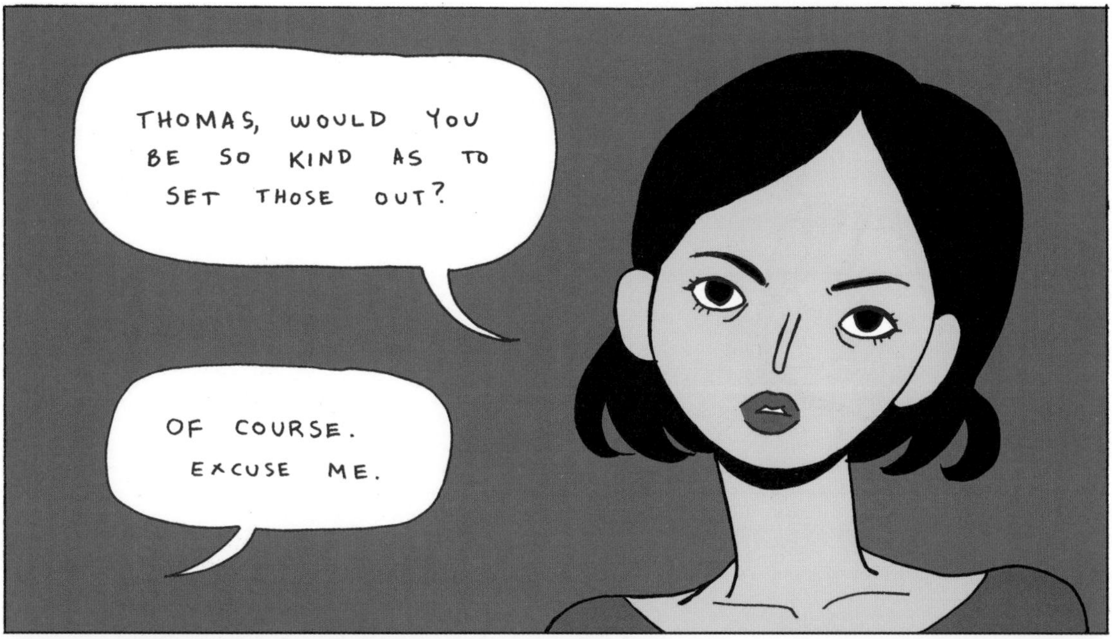
THOMAS, WOULD YOU BE SO KIND AS TO SET THOSE OUT?
OF COURSE. EXCUSE ME.

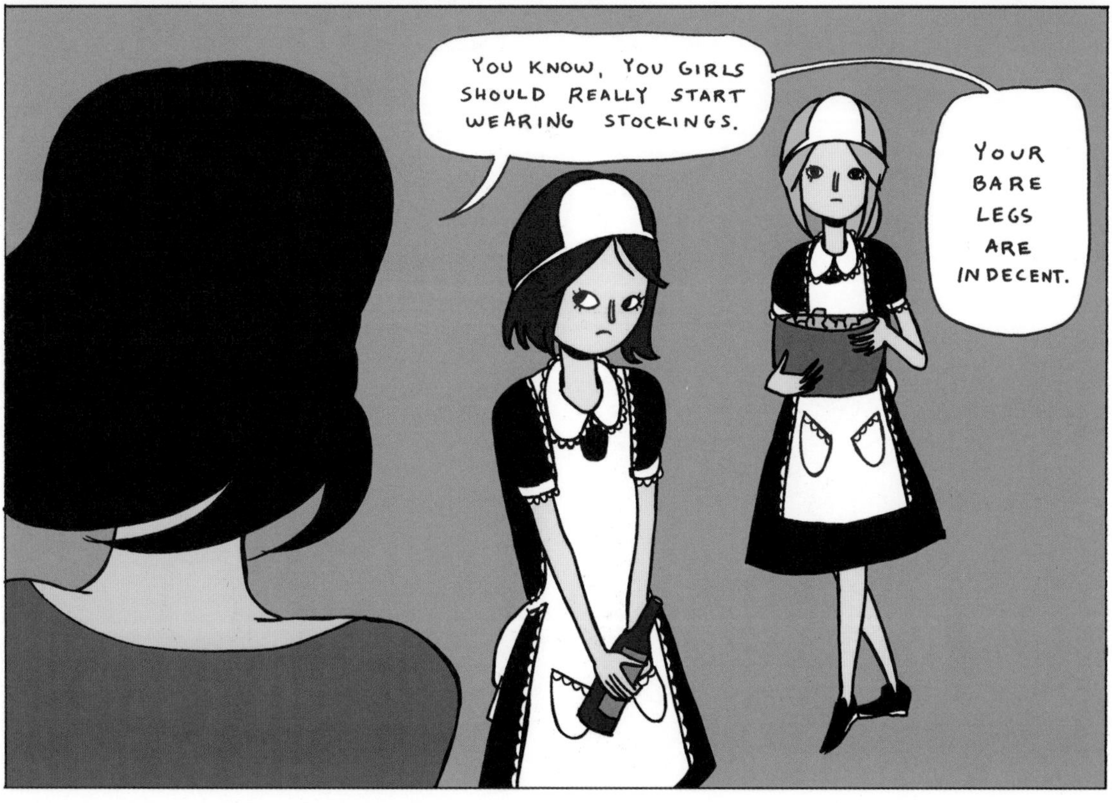
YOU KNOW, YOU GIRLS SHOULD REALLY START WEARING STOCKINGS.
YOUR BARE LEGS ARE INDECENT.

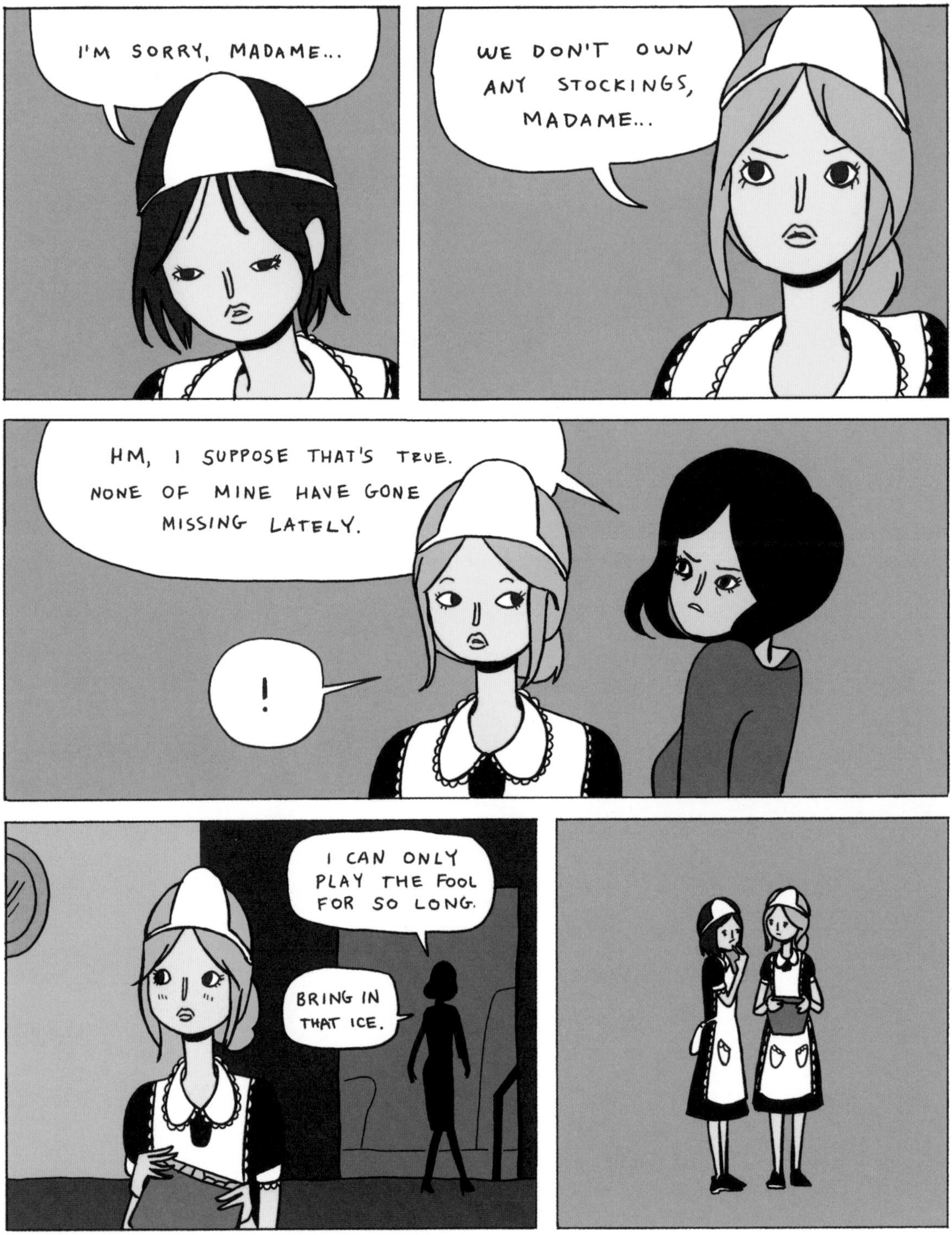
I'M SORRY, MADAME...
WE DON'T OWN ANY STOCKINGS, MADAME...
HM, I SUPPOSE THAT'S TRUE. NONE OF MINE HAVE GONE MISSING LATELY.
!
I CAN ONLY PLAY THE FOOL FOR SO LONG.
BRING IN THAT ICE.

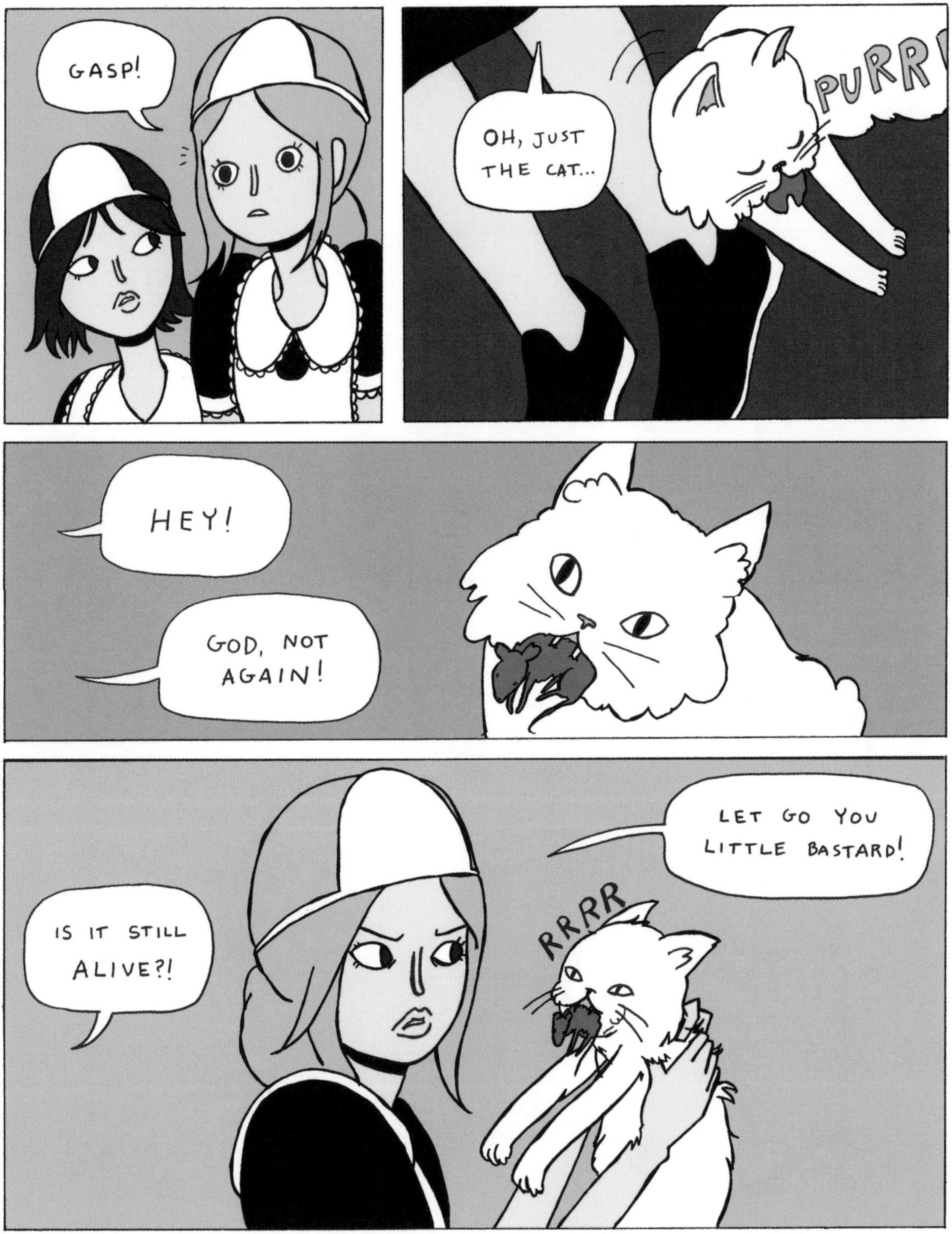
GASP!
OH, JUST THE CAT...
PURR
HEY!
GOD, NOT AGAIN!
LET GO YOU LITTLE BASTARD!
IS IT STILL ALIVE?!
RRRR

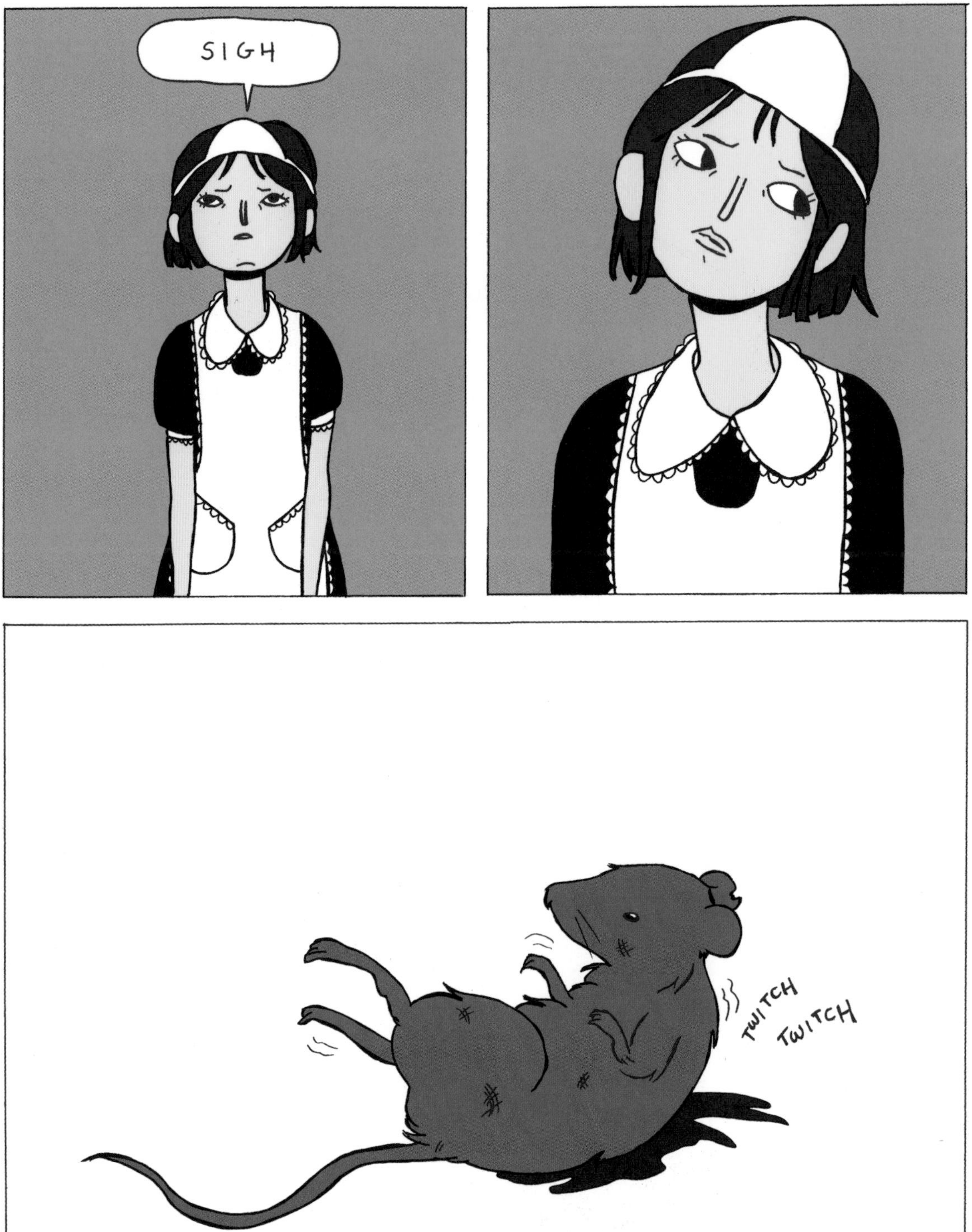
SIGH
TWITCH
TWITCH

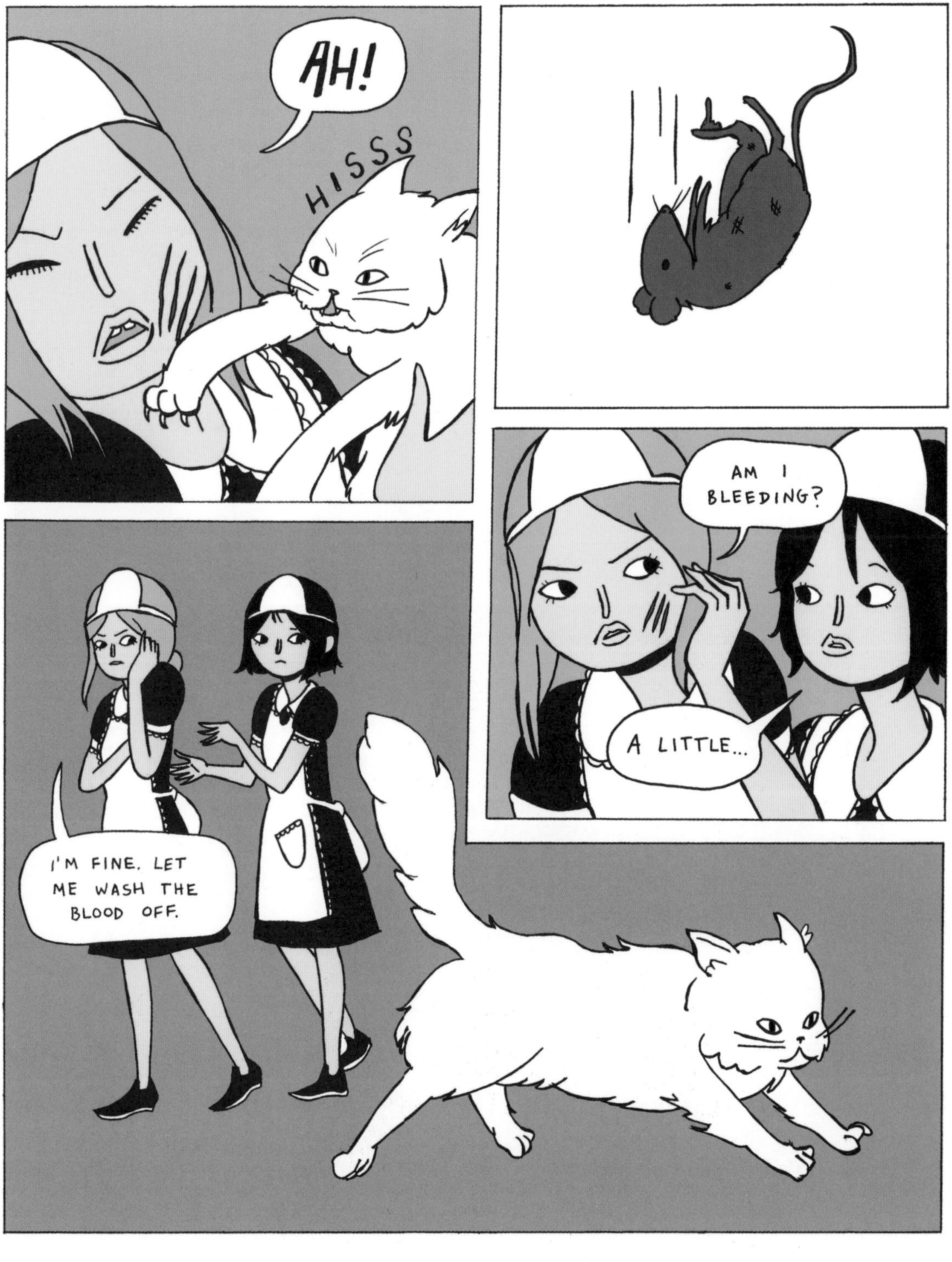
AH!
HISSS
AM I BLEEDING?
A LITTLE...
I'M FINE. LET ME WASH THE BLOOD OFF.

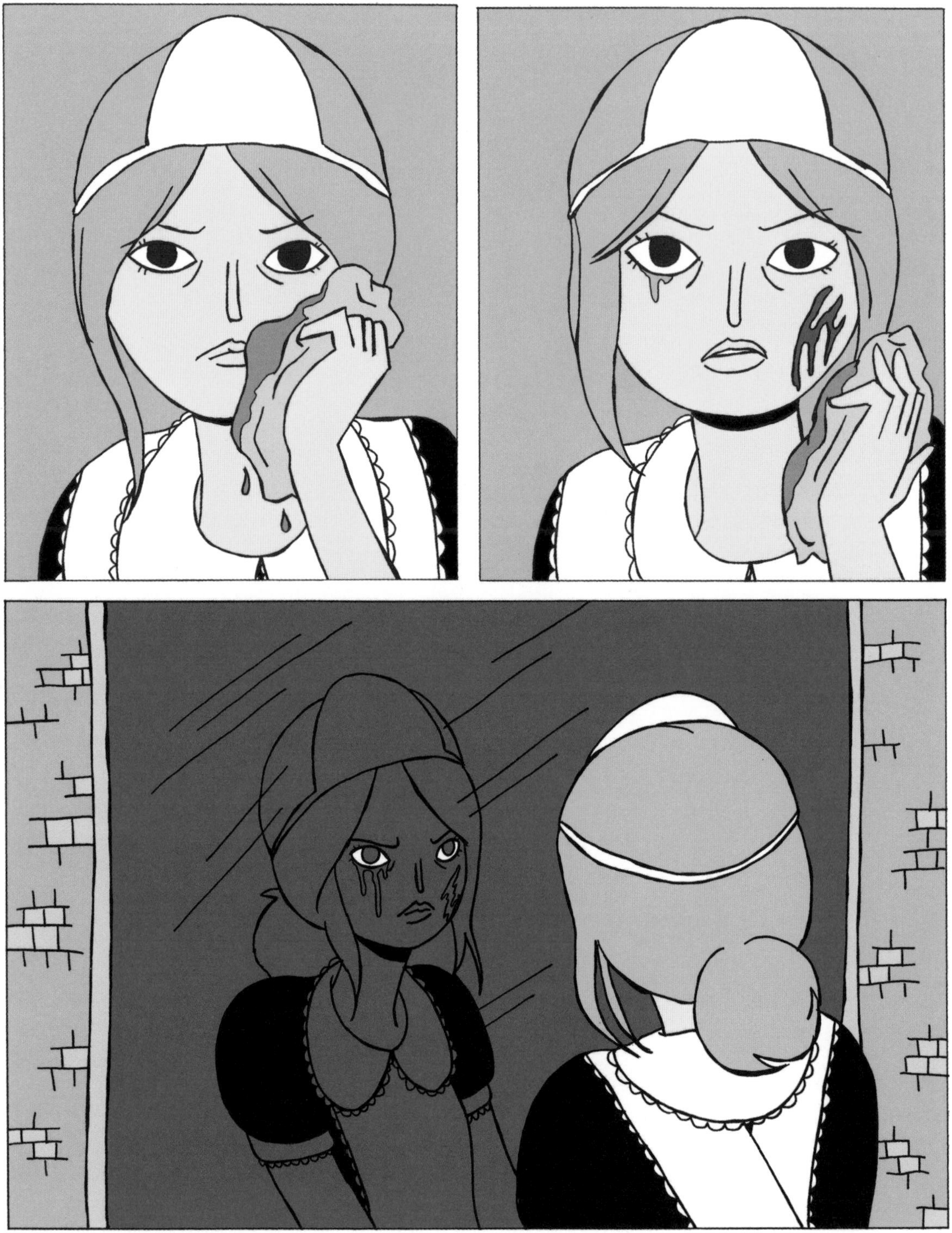

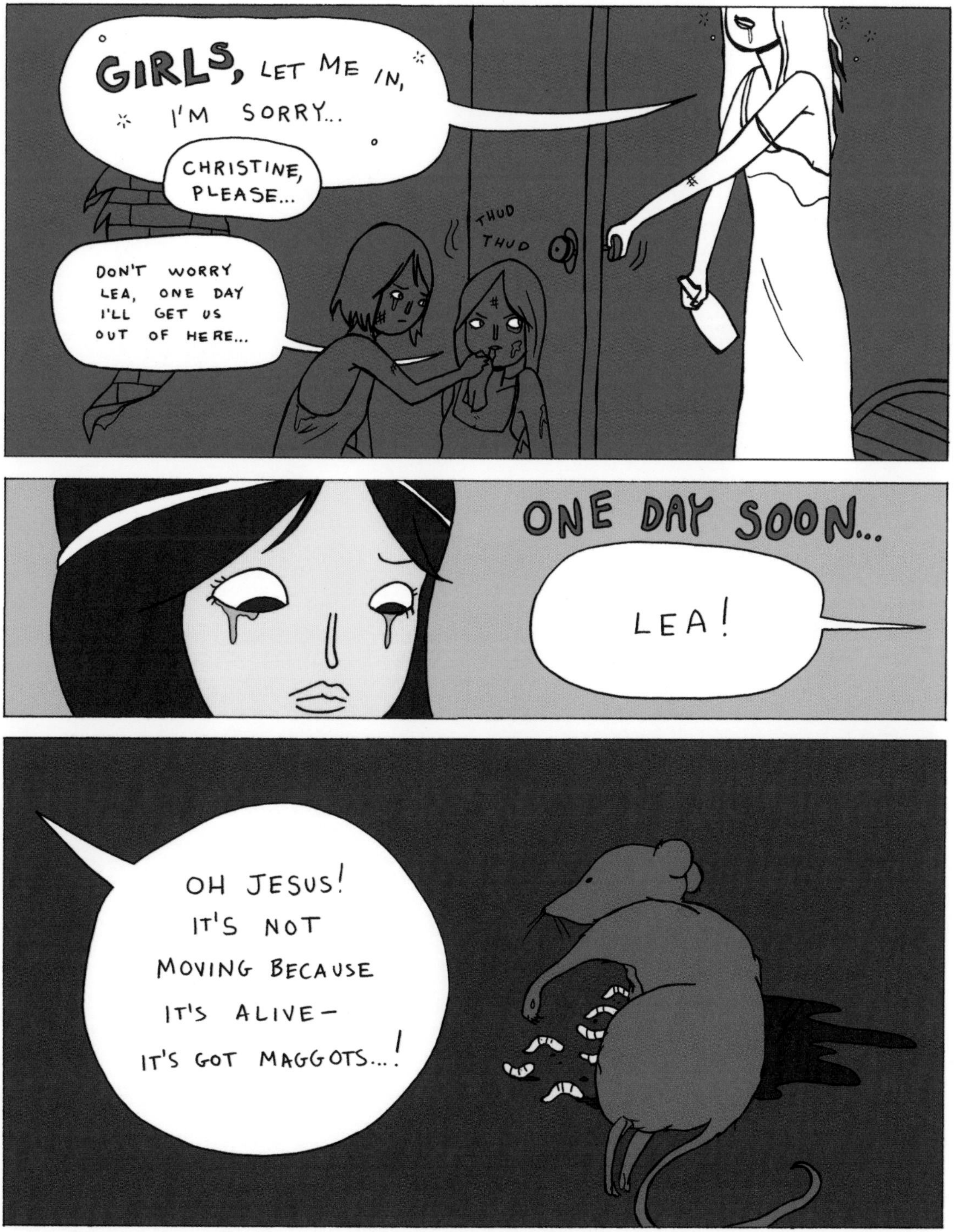
GIRLS, LET ME IN, I'M SORRY...
CHRISTINE, PLEASE...
THUD THUD
DON'T WORRY LEA, ONE DAY I'LL GET US OUT OF HERE...
ONE DAY SOON...
LEA!
OH JESUS! IT'S NOT MOVING BECAUSE IT'S ALIVE— IT'S GOT MAGGOTS...!

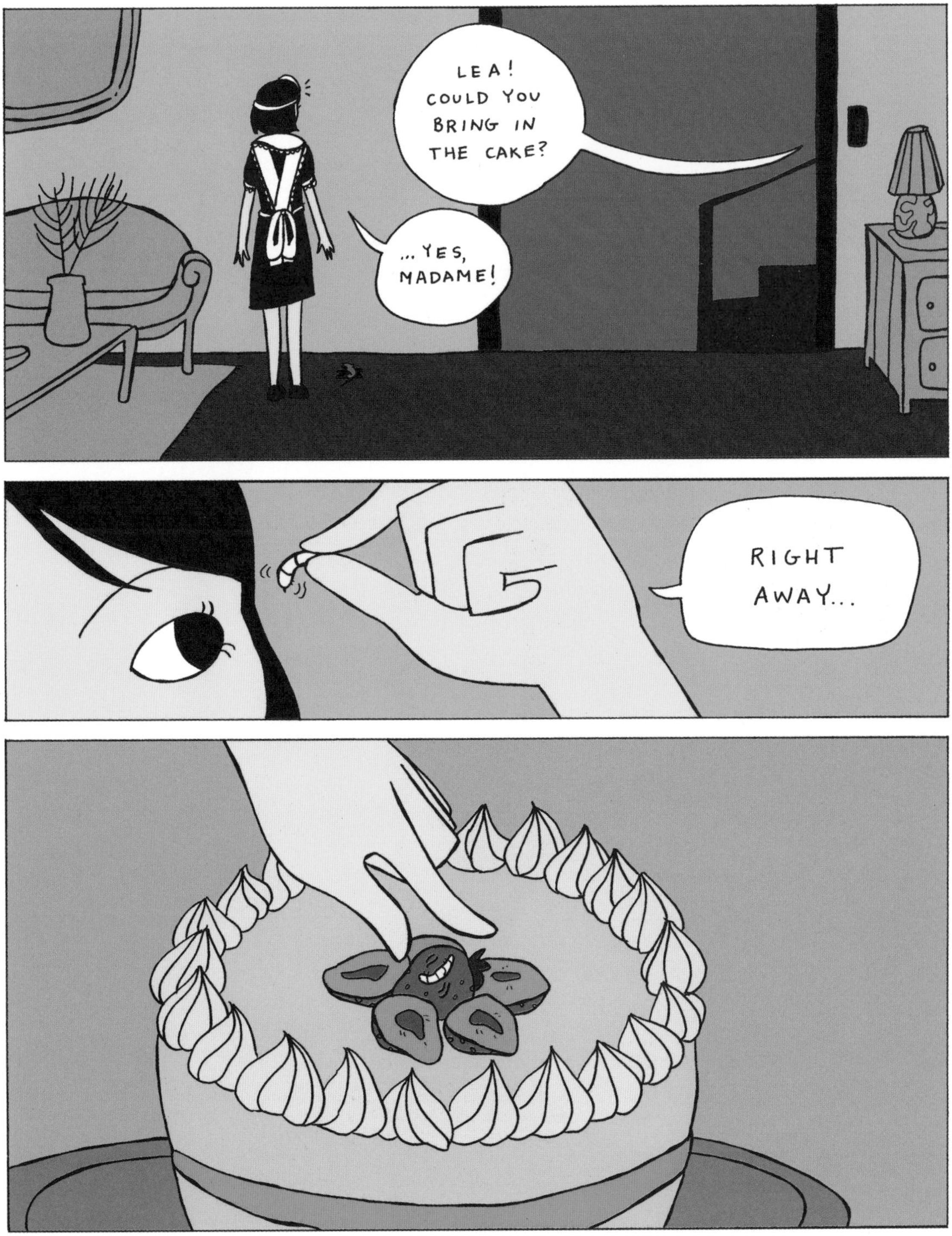

LEA! COULD YOU BRING IN THE CAKE?
...YES, MADAME!
RIGHT AWAY...

CHAPTER

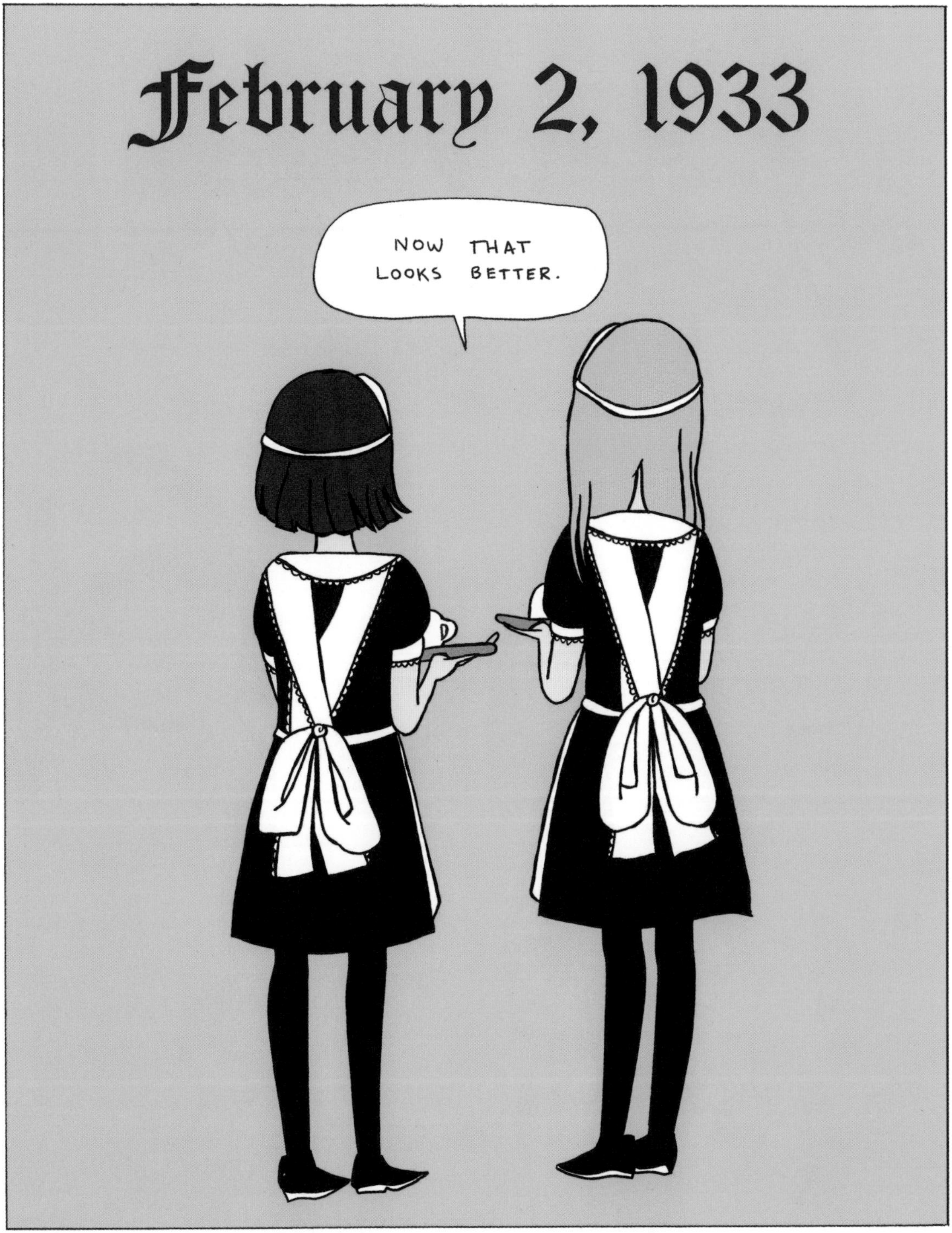
February 2, 1933
NOW THAT LOOKS BETTER.

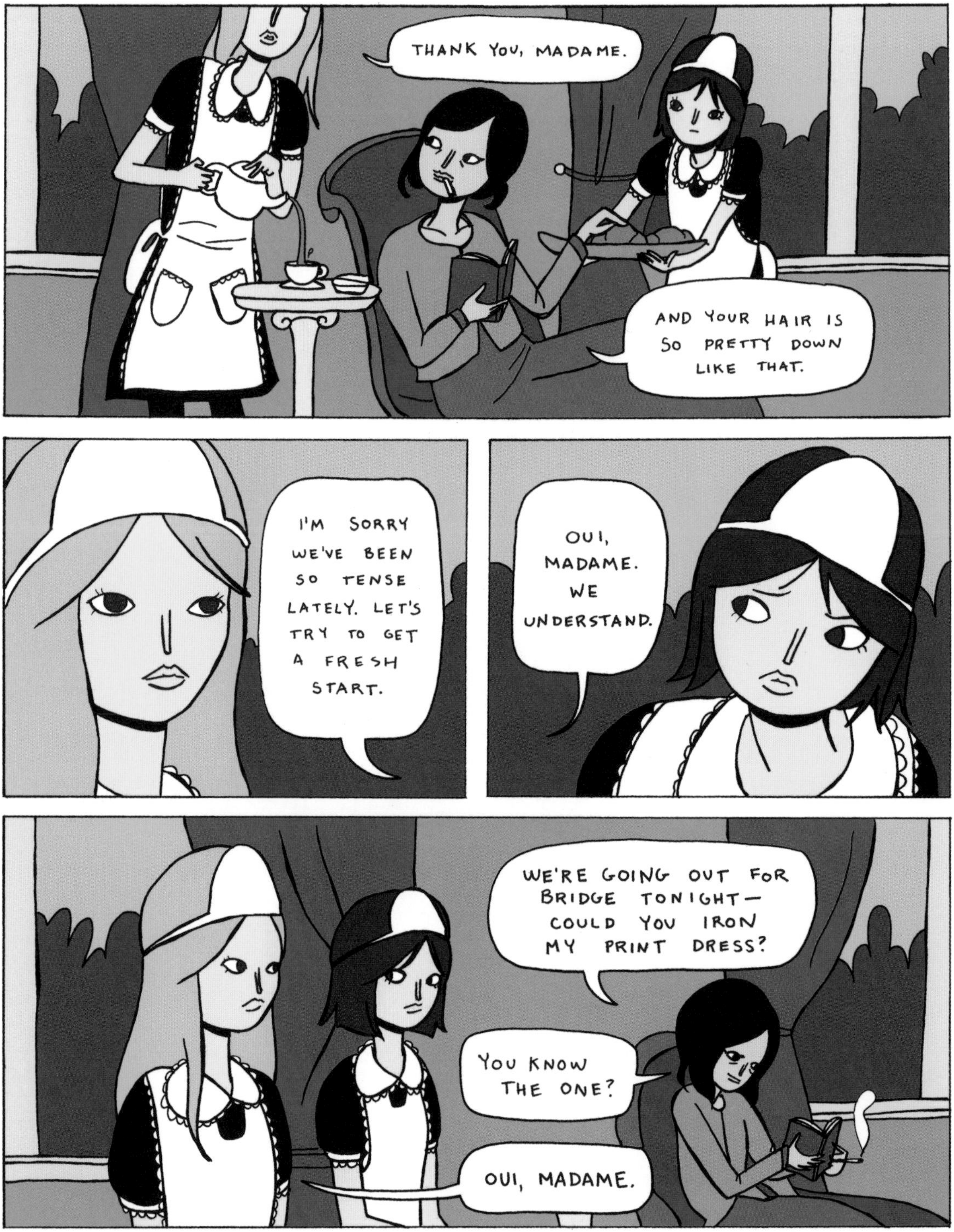
THANK YOU, MADAME.
AND YOUR HAIR IS SO PRETTY DOWN LIKE THAT.
I'M SORRY WE'VE BEEN SO TENSE LATELY. LET'S TRY TO GET A FRESH START.
OUI, MADAME. WE UNDERSTAND.
WE'RE GOING OUT FOR BRIDGE TONIGHT— COULD YOU IRON MY PRINT DRESS?
YOU KNOW THE ONE?
OUI, MADAME.

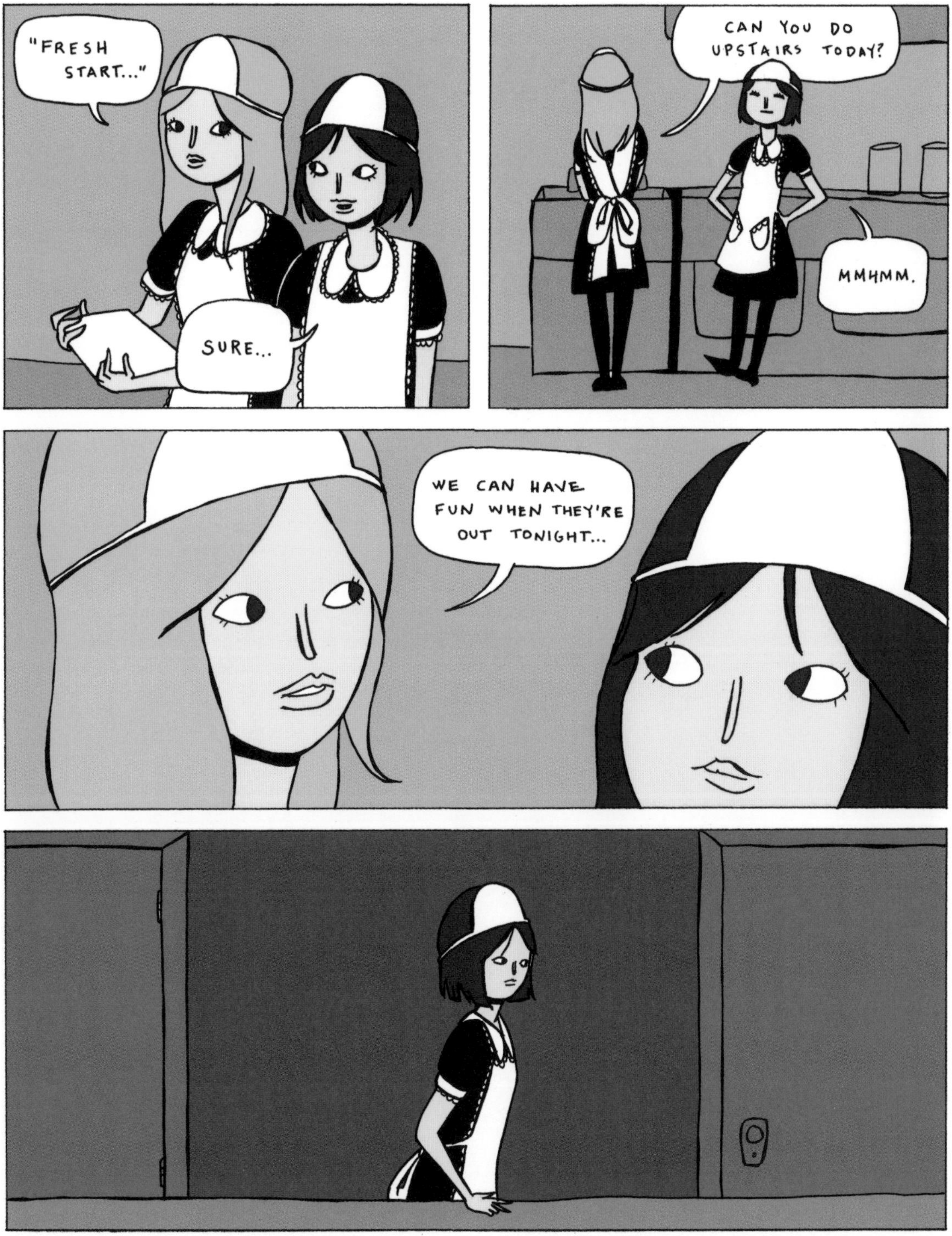
"FRESH START..."
SURE...
CAN YOU DO UPSTAIRS TODAY?
MMHMM.
WE CAN HAVE FUN WHEN THEY'RE OUT TONIGHT...

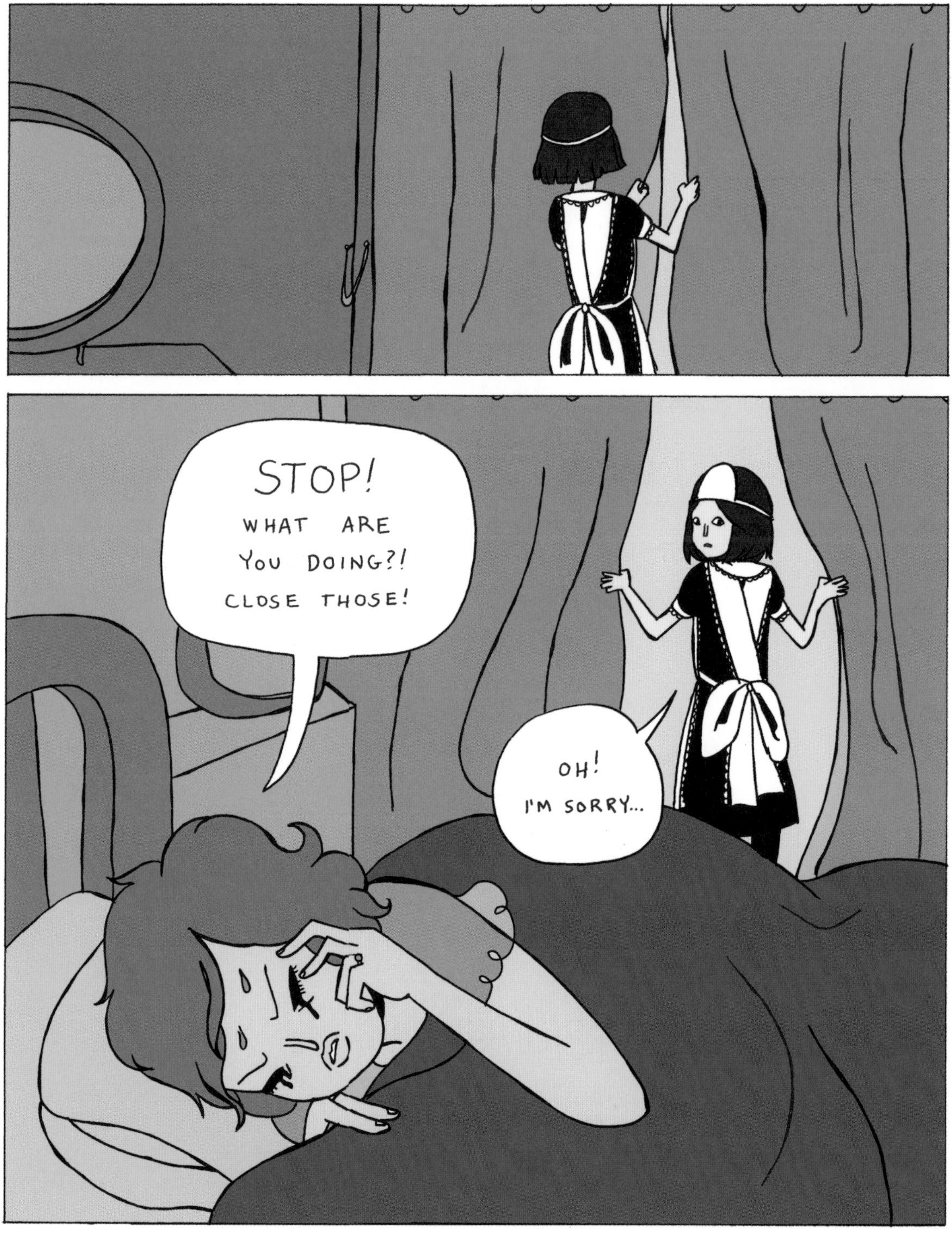
STOP! WHAT ARE YOU DOING?! CLOSE THOSE!
OH! I'M SORRY...

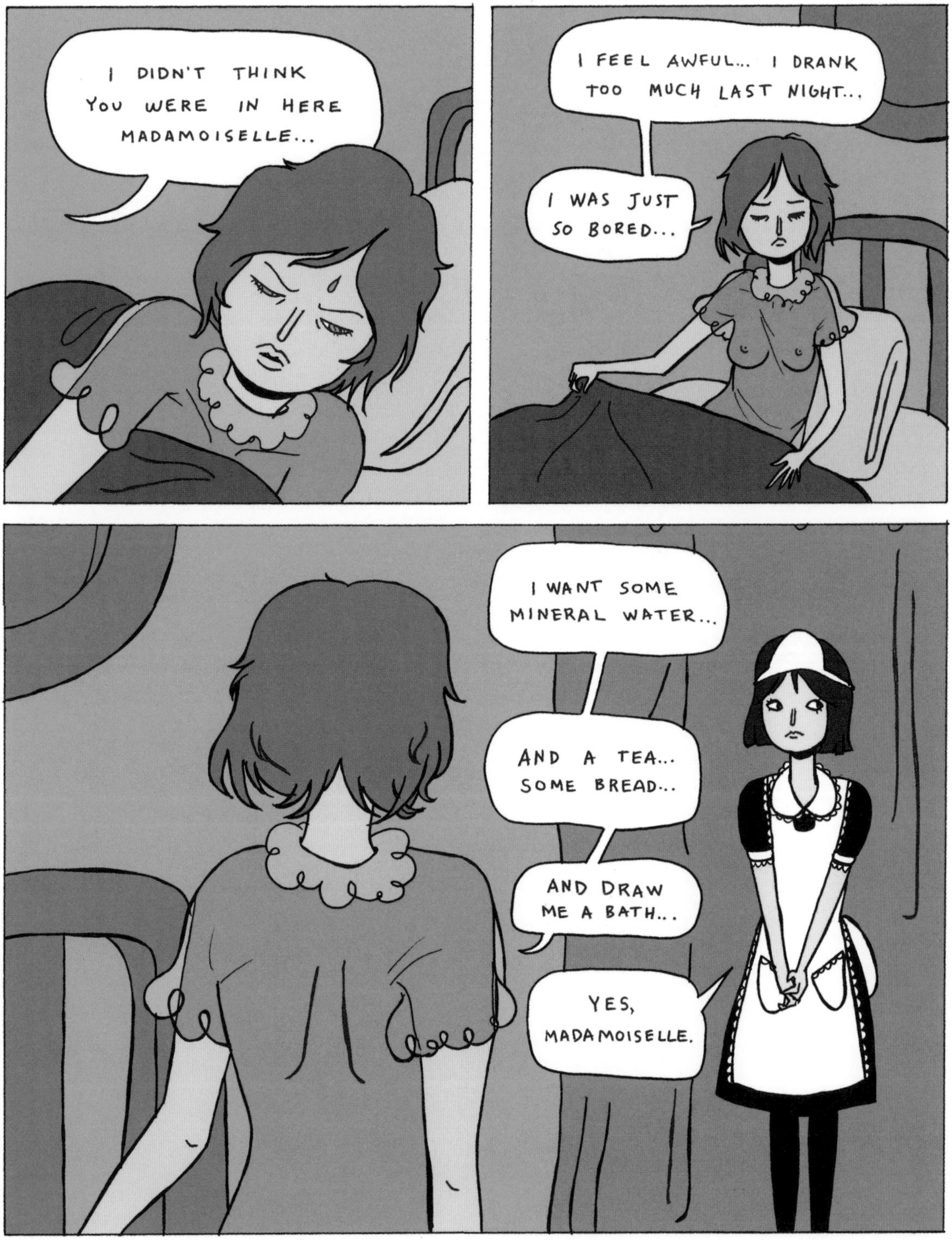
I DIDN'T THINK YOU WERE IN HERE MADAMOISELLE...
I FEEL AWFUL... I DRANK TOO MUCH LAST NIGHT...
I WAS JUST SO BORED...
I WANT SOME MINERAL WATER...
AND A TEA... SOME BREAD...
AND DRAW ME A BATH...
YES, MADAMOISELLE.

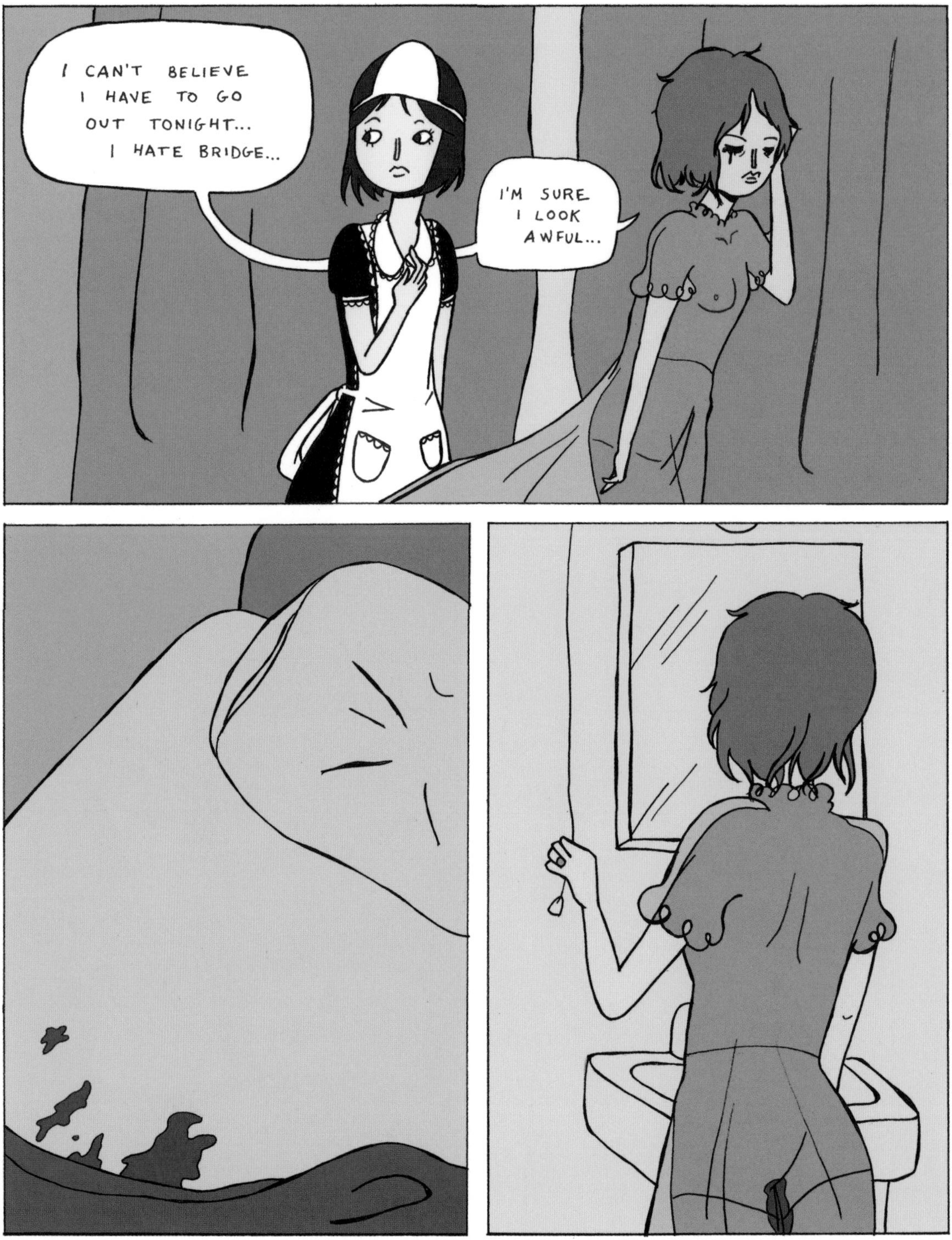
I CAN'T BELIEVE I HAVE TO GO OUT TONIGHT... I HATE BRIDGE...
I'M SURE I LOOK AWFUL...

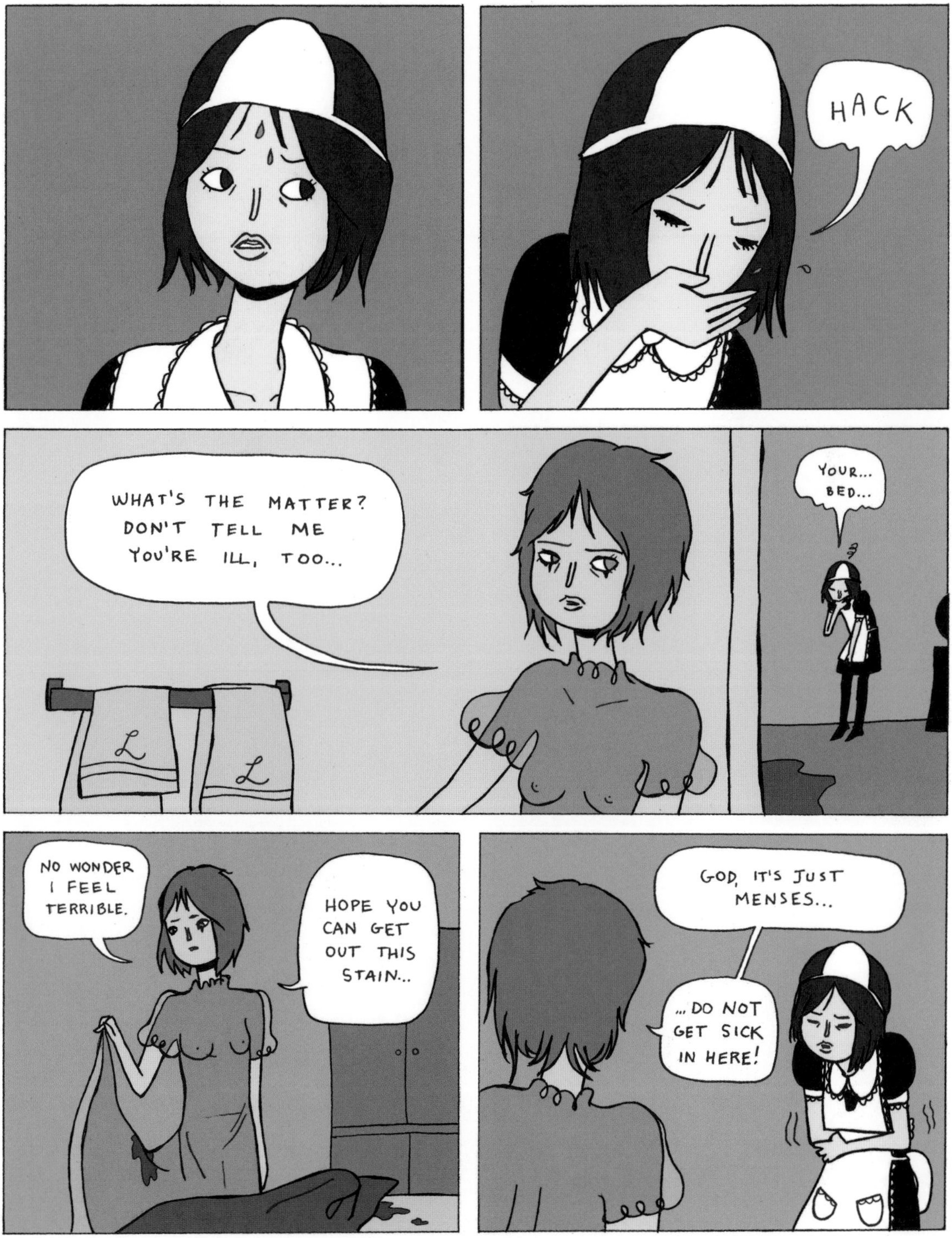
HACK
WHAT'S THE MATTER? DON'T TELL ME YOU'RE ILL, TOO...
YOUR... BED...
NO WONDER I FEEL TERRIBLE.
HOPE YOU CAN GET OUT THIS STAIN...
GOD, IT'S JUST MENSES...
...DO NOT GET SICK IN HERE!

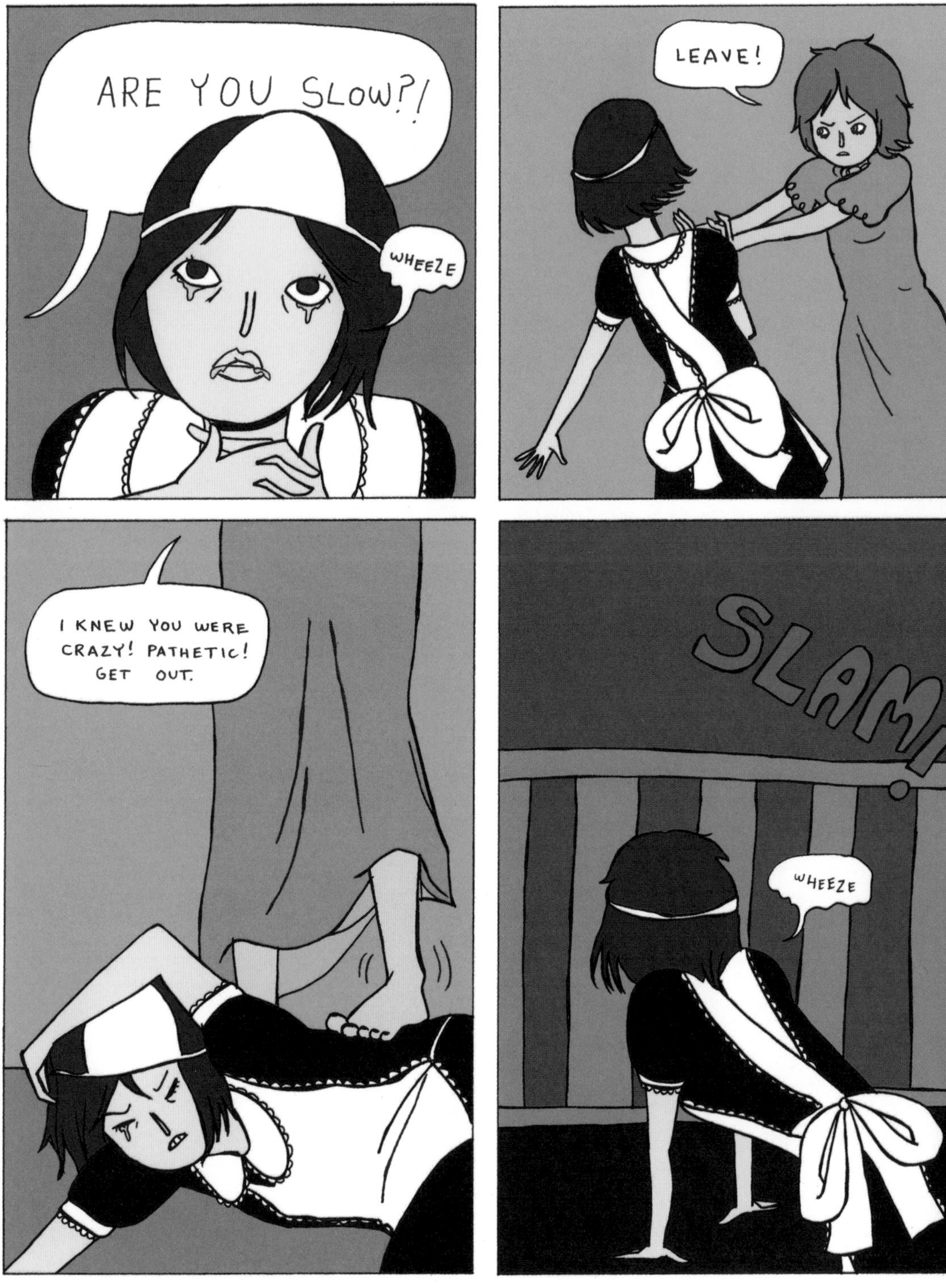
ARE YOU SLOW?!
WHEEZE
LEAVE!
I KNEW YOU WERE CRAZY! PATHETIC! GET OUT.
SLAM!
WHEEZE

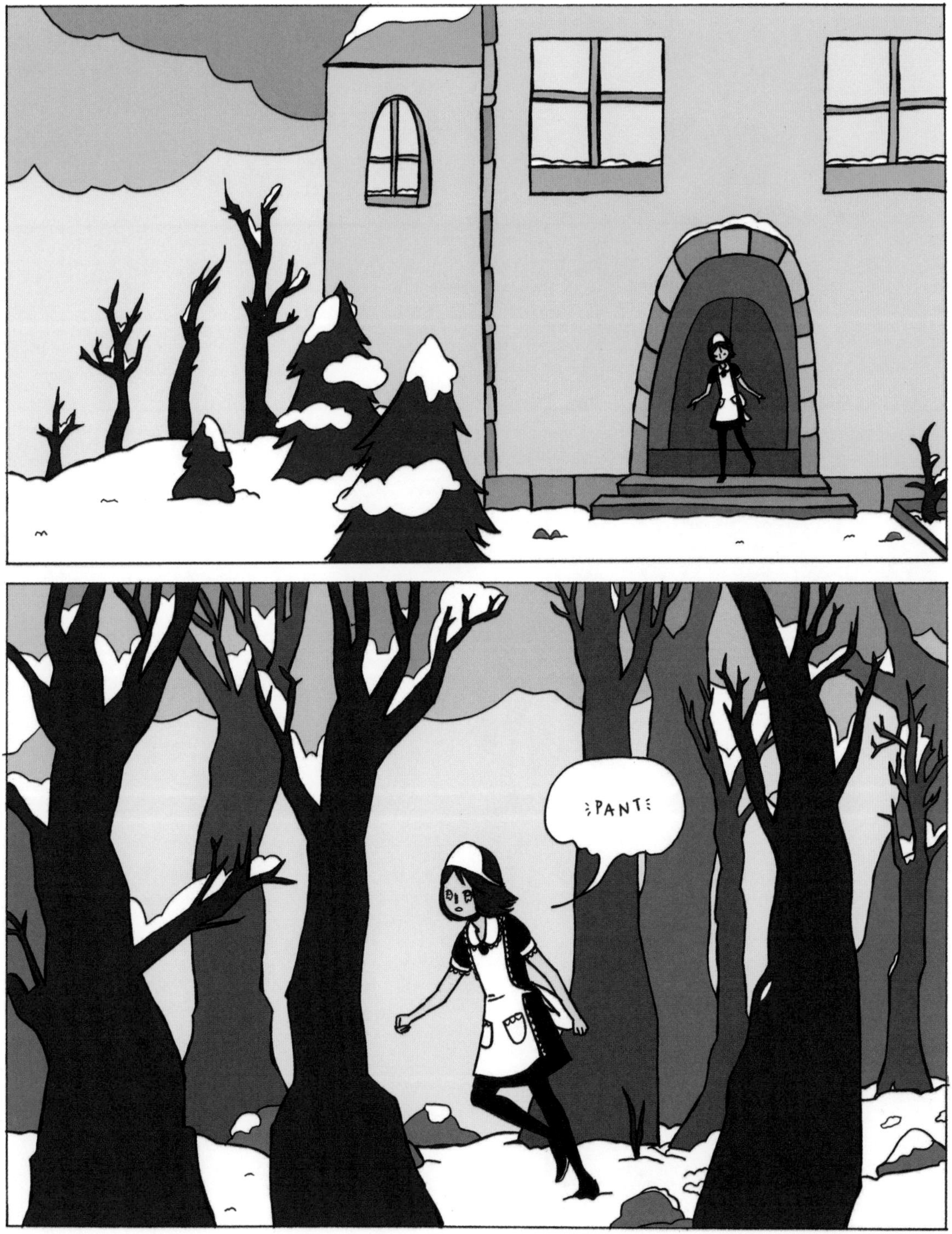
PANT

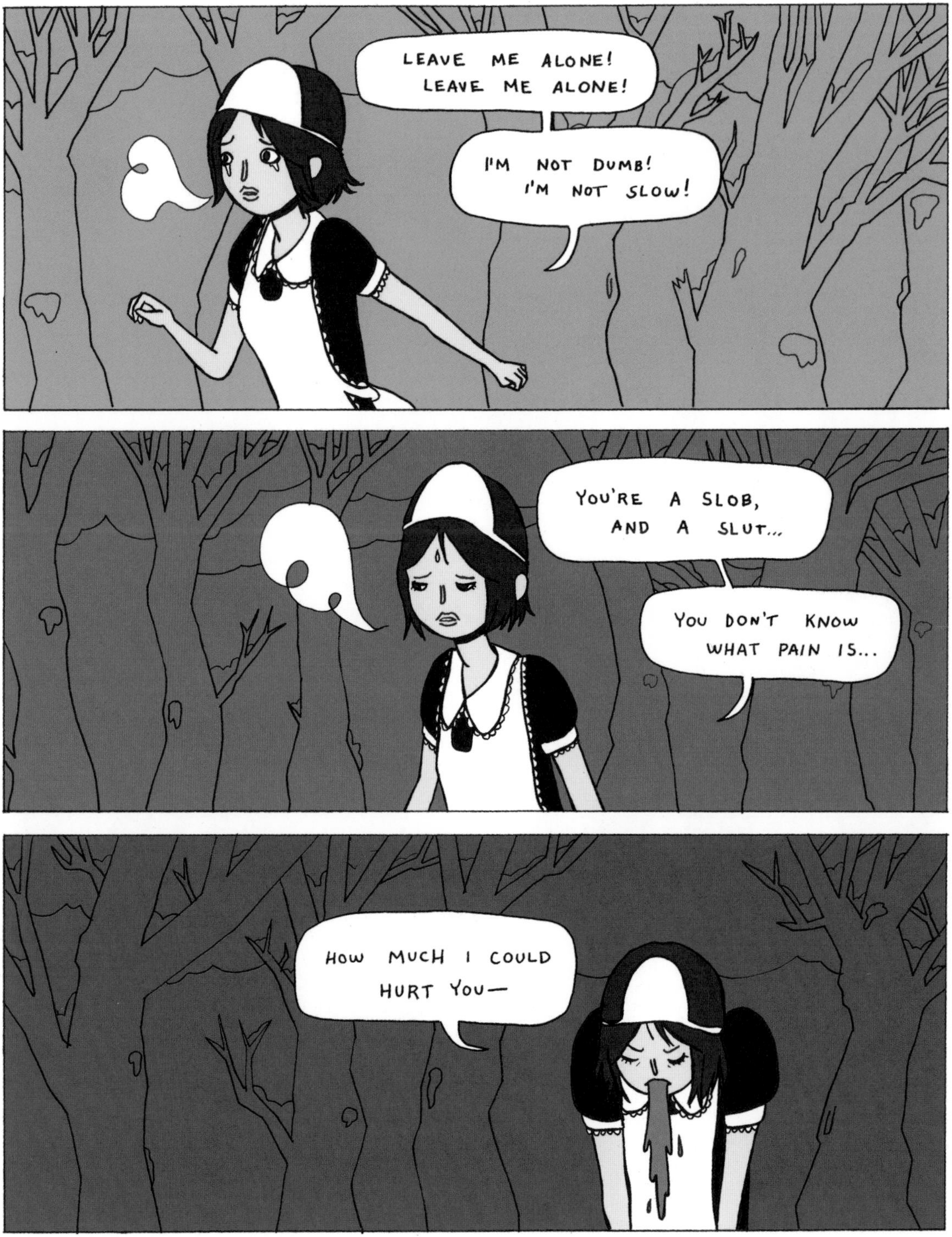
LEAVE ME ALONE! LEAVE ME ALONE!
I'M NOT DUMB! I'M NOT SLOW!
YOU'RE A SLOB, AND A SLUT...
YOU DON'T KNOW WHAT PAIN IS...
HOW MUCH I COULD HURT YOU—

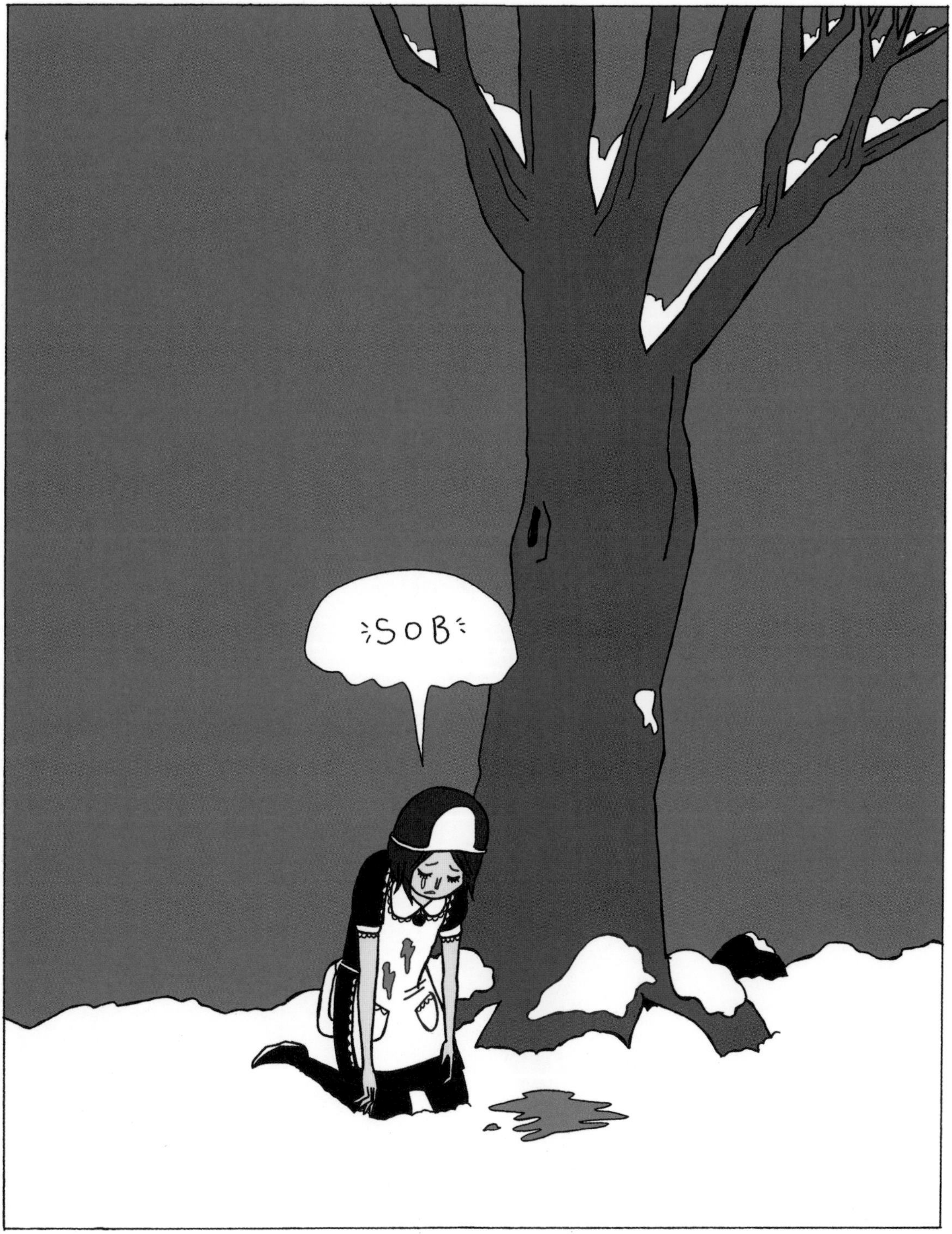
SOB

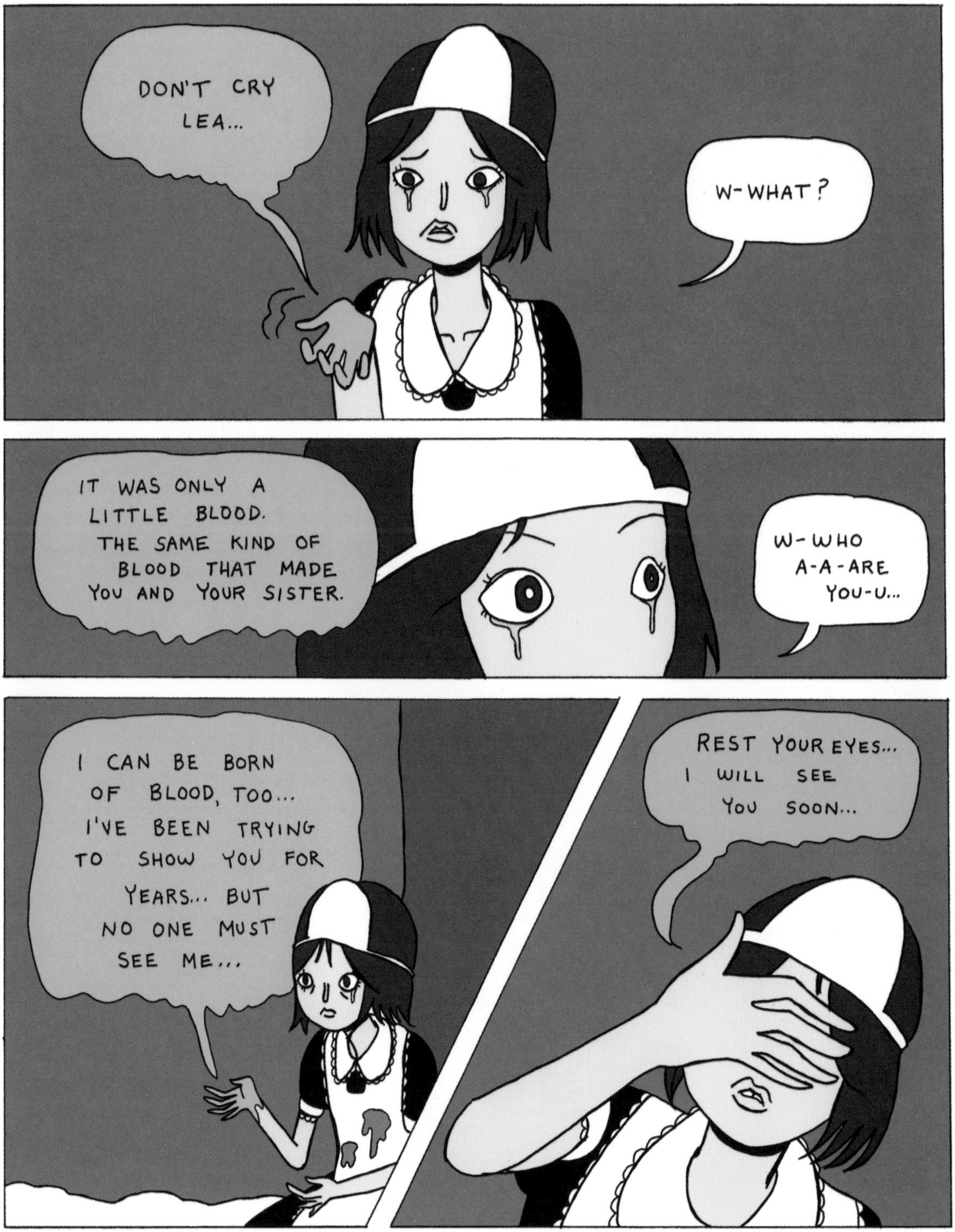
DON'T CRY LEA...
W-WHAT?
IT WAS ONLY A LITTLE BLOOD. THE SAME KIND OF BLOOD THAT MADE YOU AND YOUR SISTER.
W-WHO A-A-ARE YOU-U...
I CAN BE BORN OF BLOOD, TOO... I'VE BEEN TRYING TO SHOW YOU FOR YEARS... BUT NO ONE MUST SEE ME...
REST YOUR EYES... I WILL SEE YOU SOON...

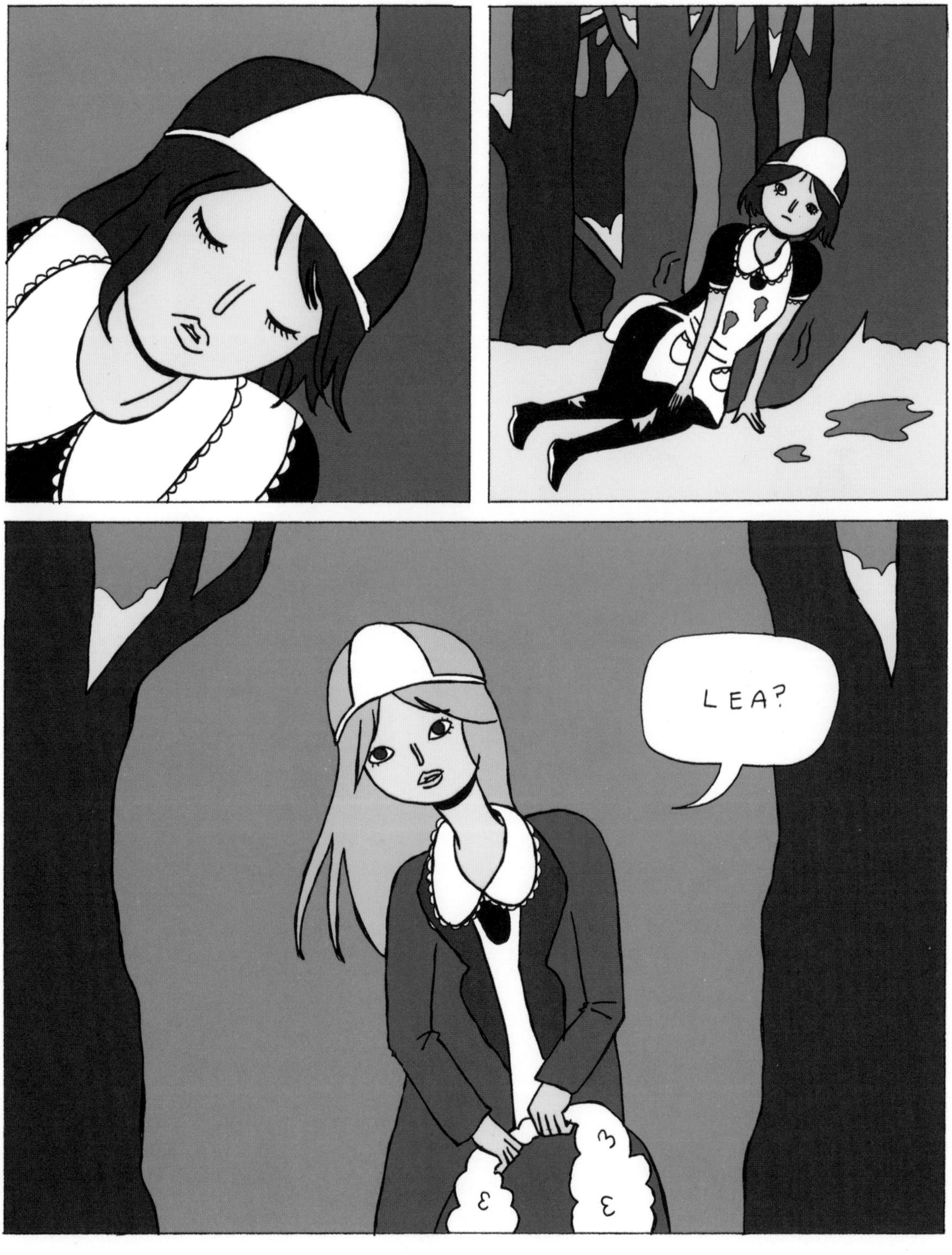
LEA?

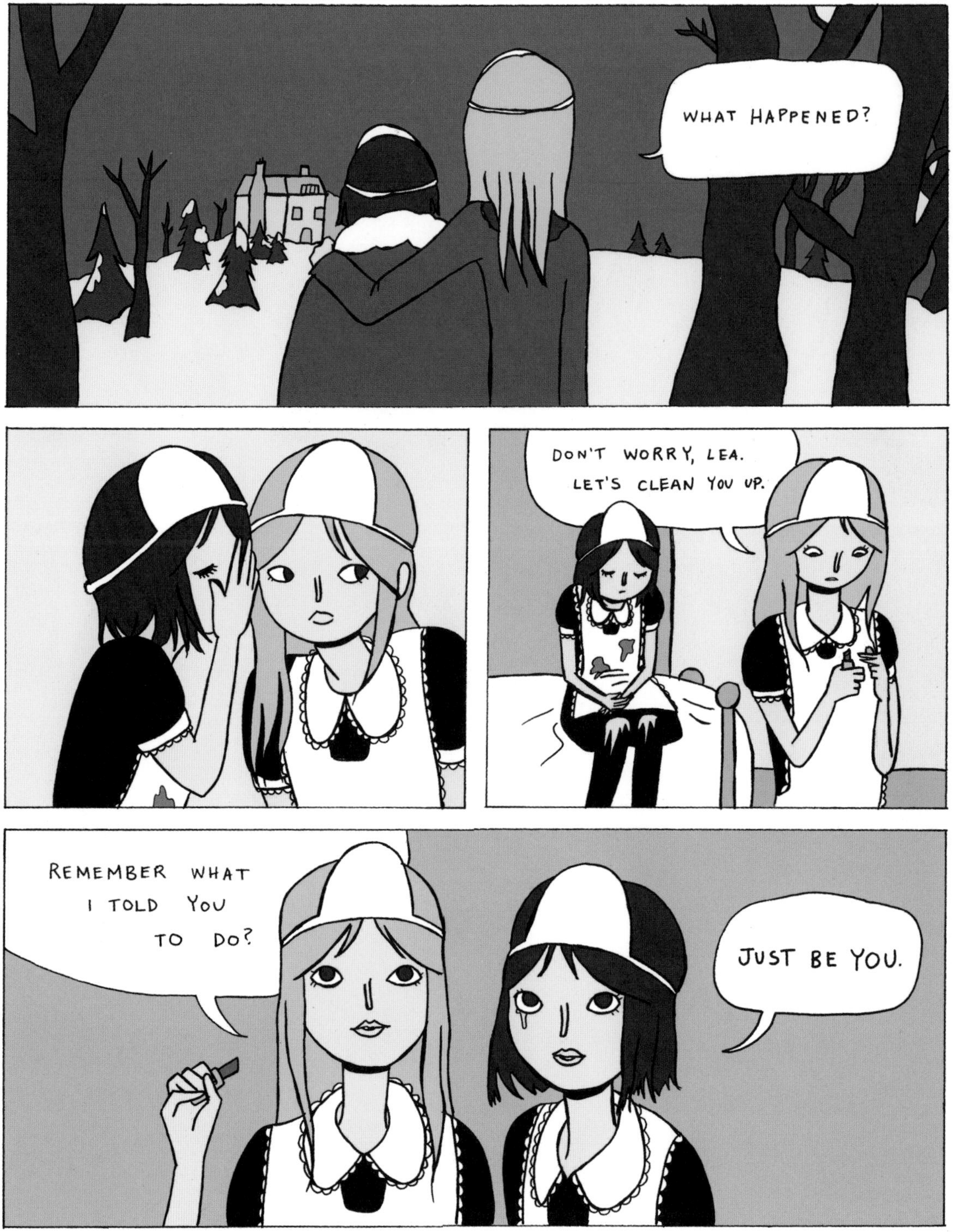
WHAT HAPPENED?
DON'T WORRY, LEA. LET'S CLEAN YOU UP.
REMEMBER WHAT I TOLD YOU TO DO?
JUST BE YOU.

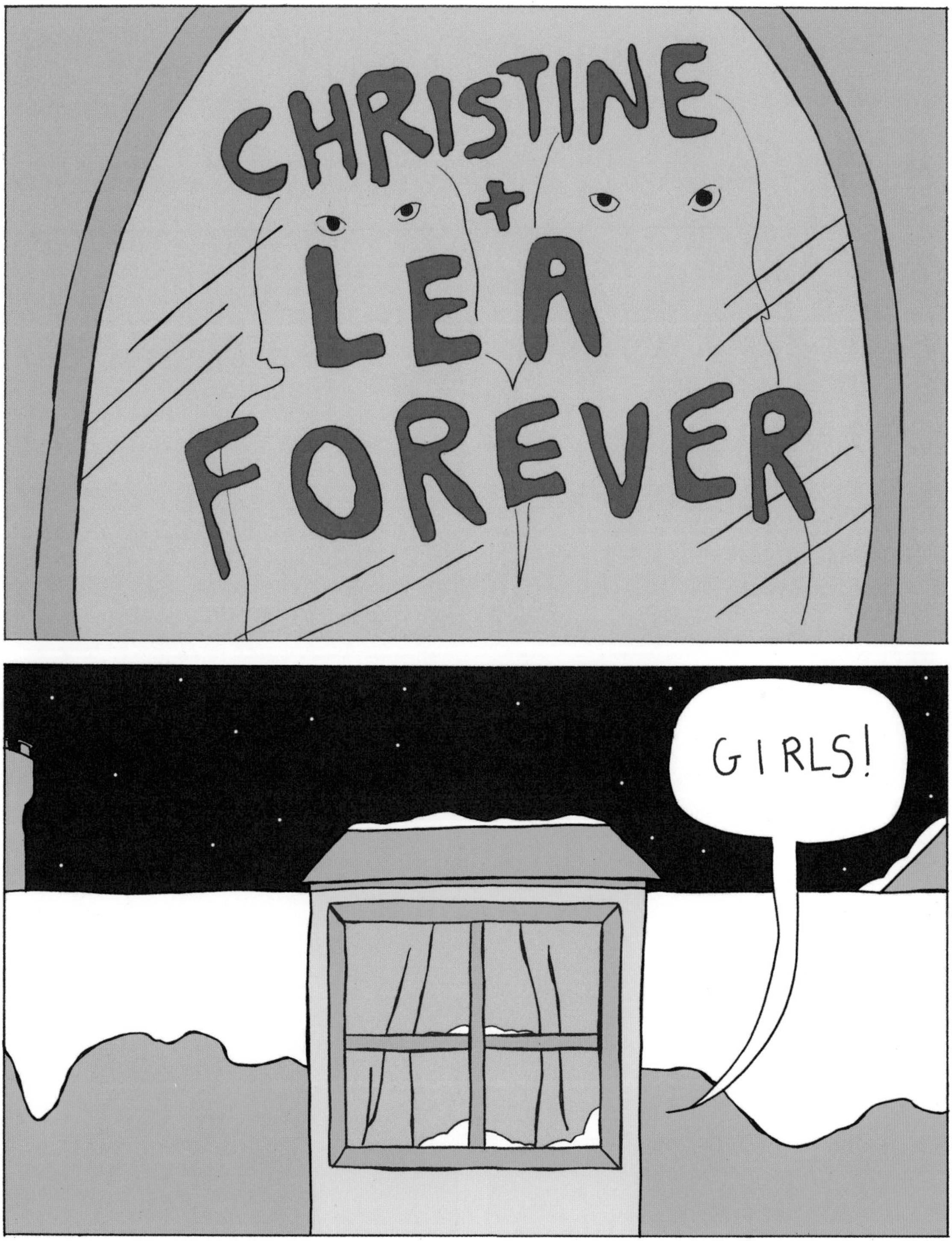
CHRISTINE + LEA FOREVER
GIRLS!

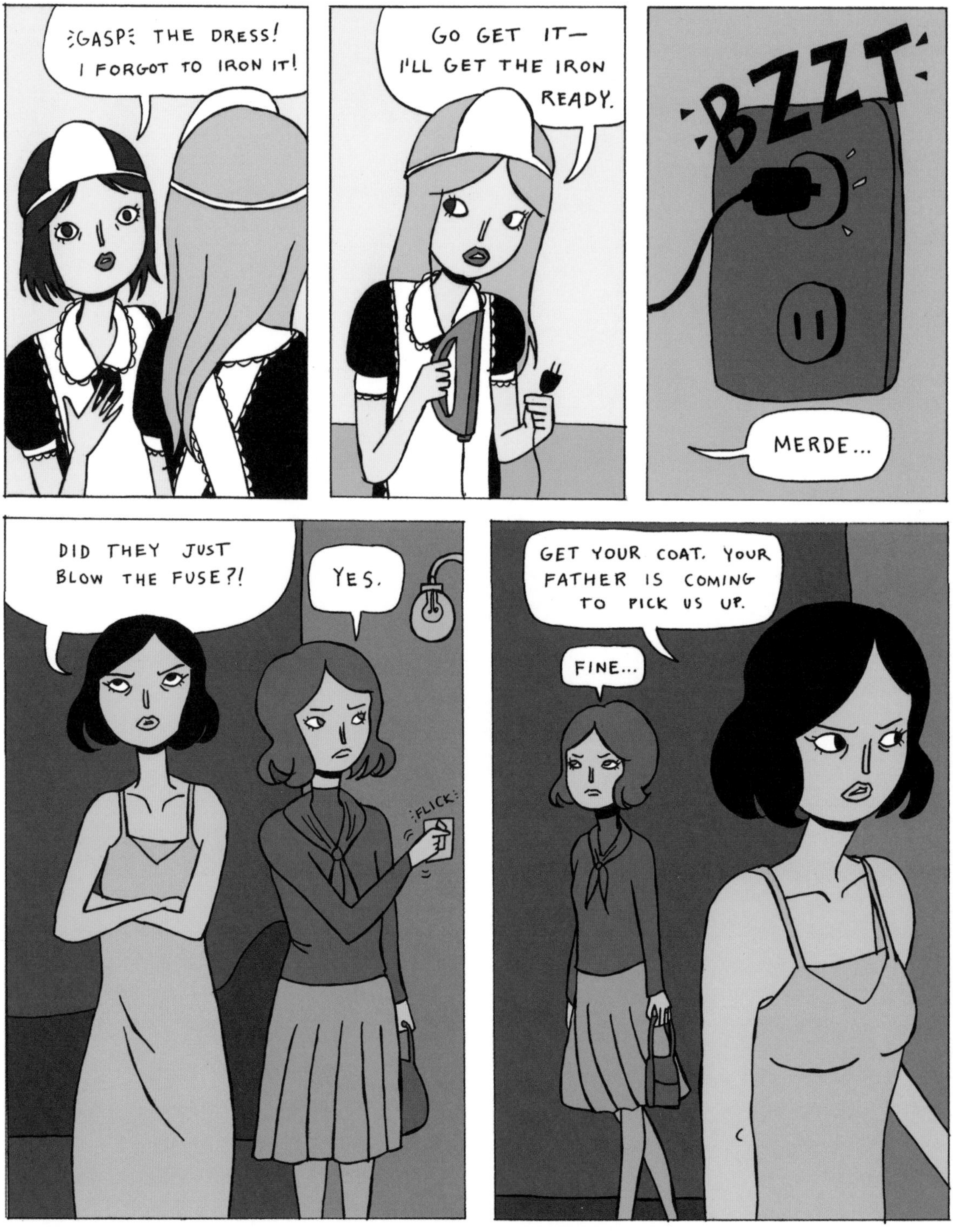

:GASP: THE DRESS! I FORGOT TO IRON IT!
GO GET IT— I'LL GET THE IRON READY.
BZZT
MERDE...
DID THEY JUST BLOW THE FUSE?!
YES.
:FLICK:
GET YOUR COAT. YOUR FATHER IS COMING TO PICK US UP.
FINE...

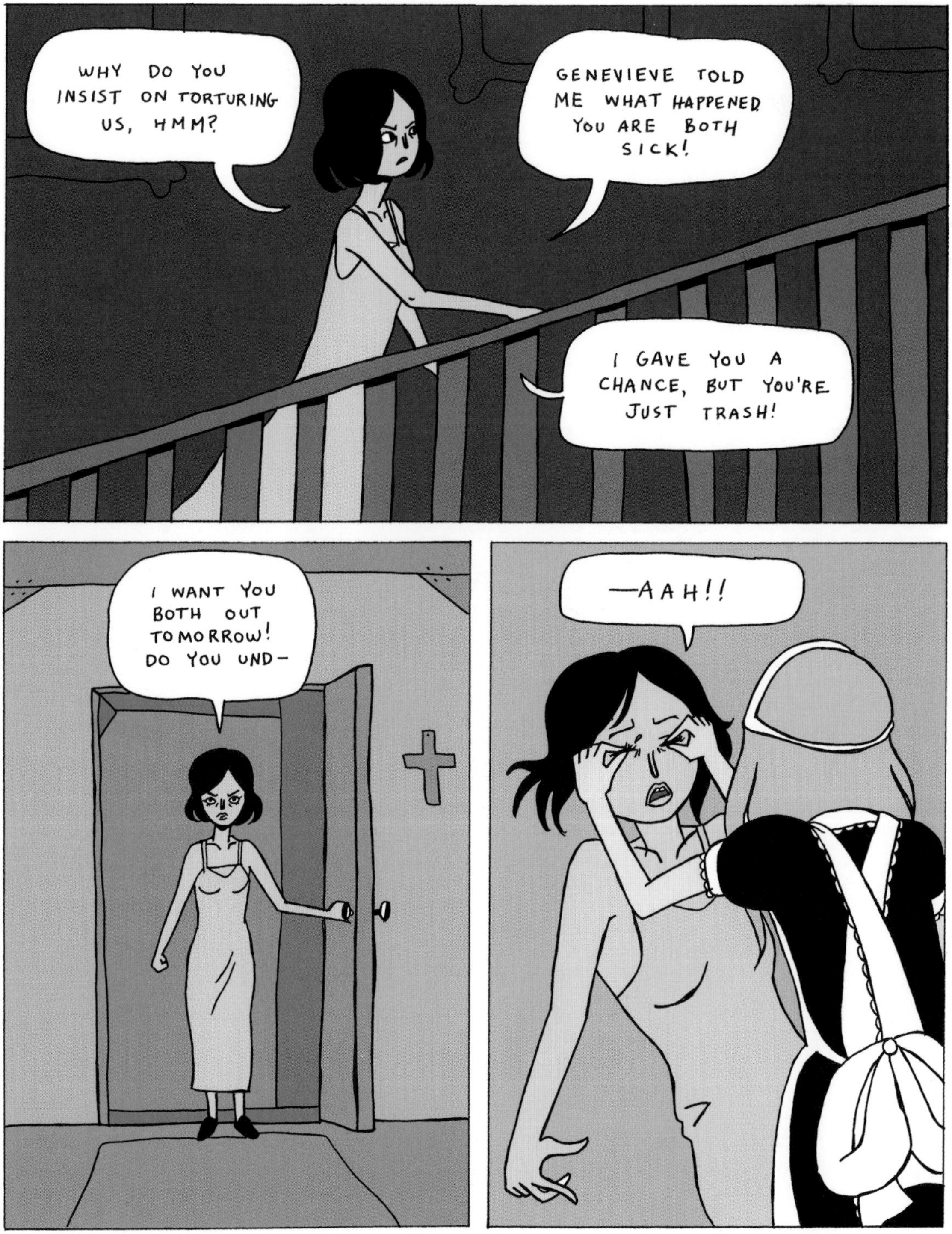
WHY DO YOU INSIST ON TORTURING US, HMM?
GENEVIEVE TOLD ME WHAT HAPPENED. YOU ARE BOTH SICK!
I GAVE YOU A CHANCE, BUT YOU'RE JUST TRASH!
I WANT YOU BOTH OUT TOMORROW! DO YOU UND–
—AAH!!

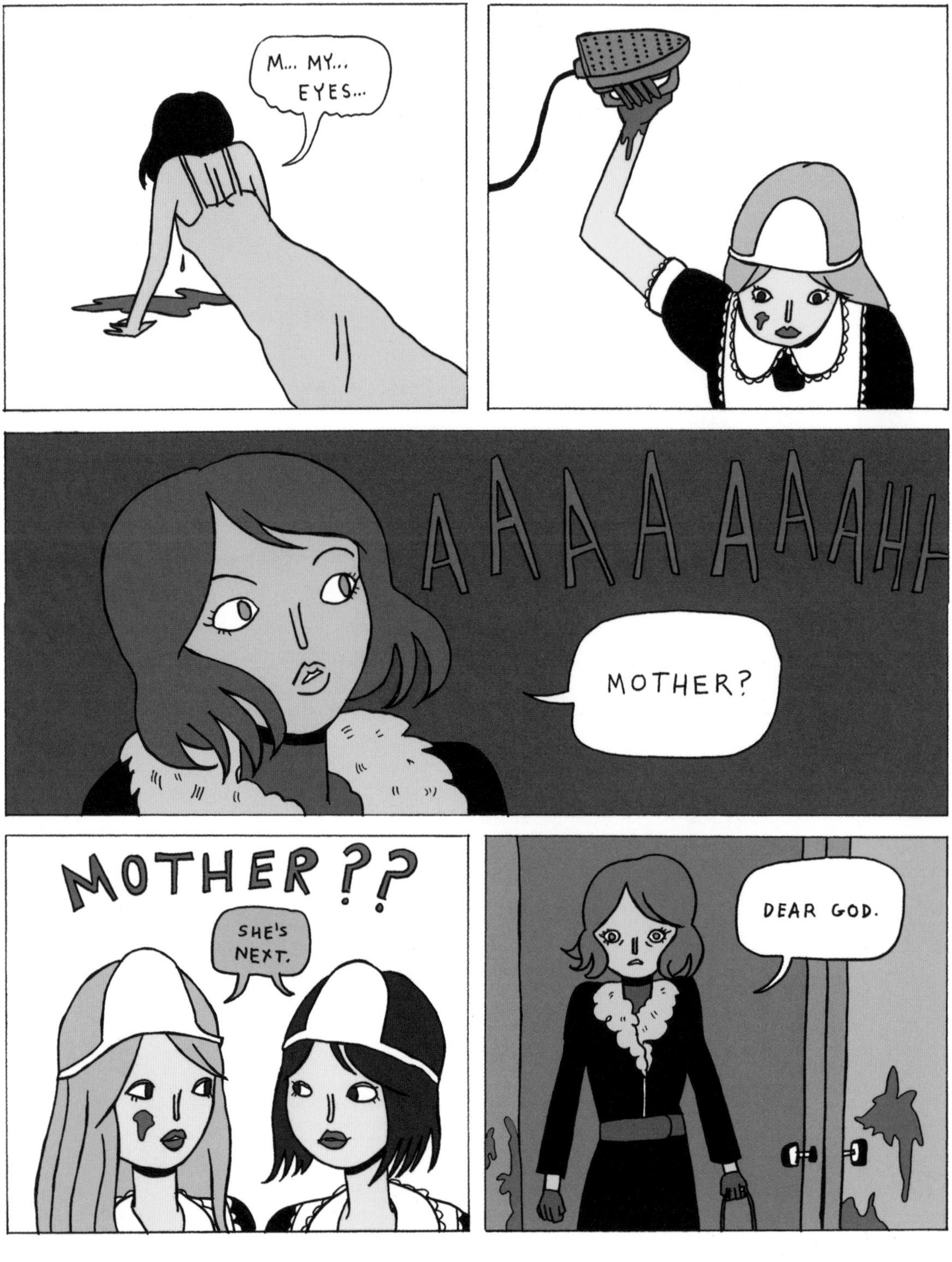
M... MY... EYES...
AAAAAAAHH
MOTHER?
MOTHER??
SHE'S NEXT.
DEAR GOD.

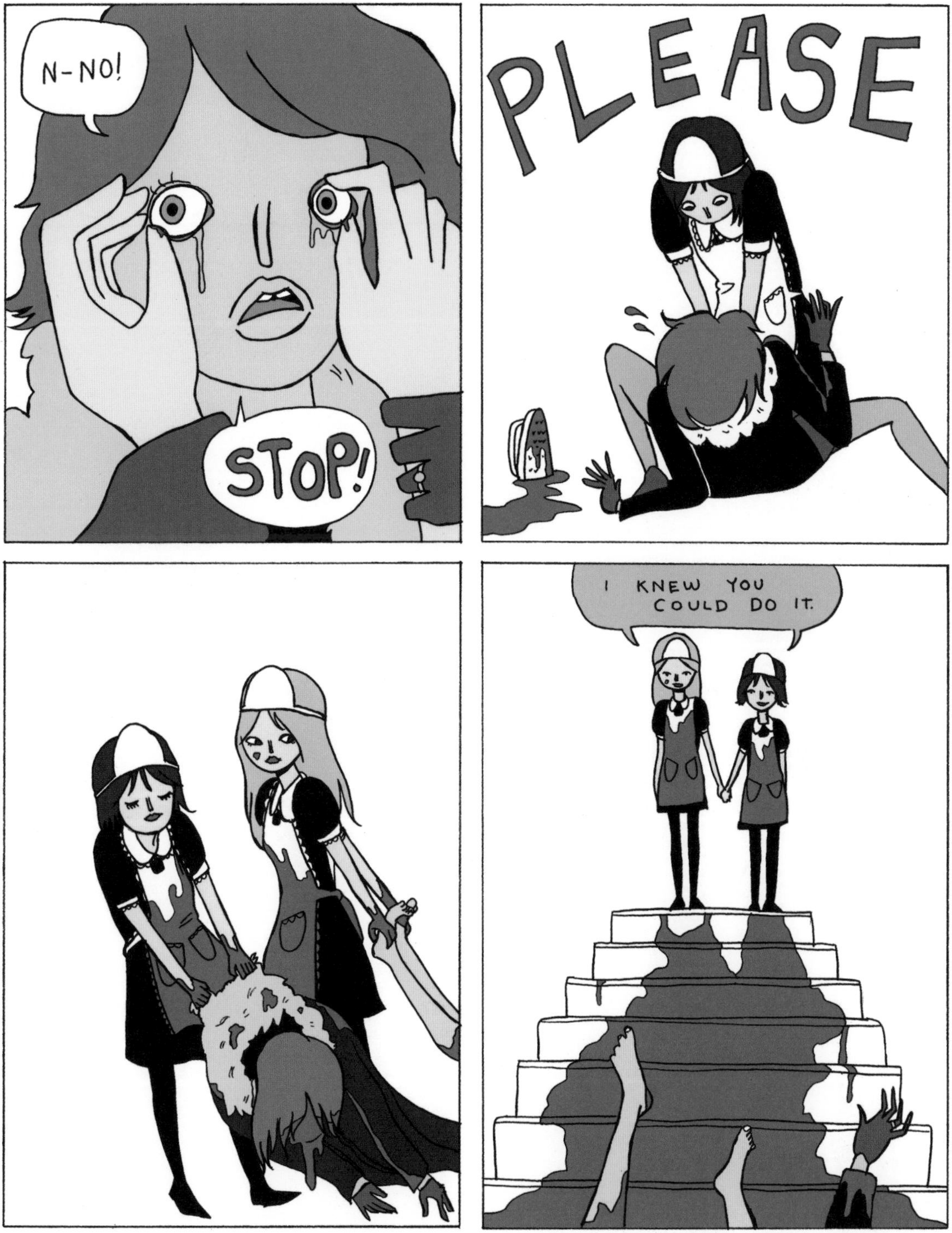
N-NO!
STOP!
PLEASE
I KNEW YOU COULD DO IT.

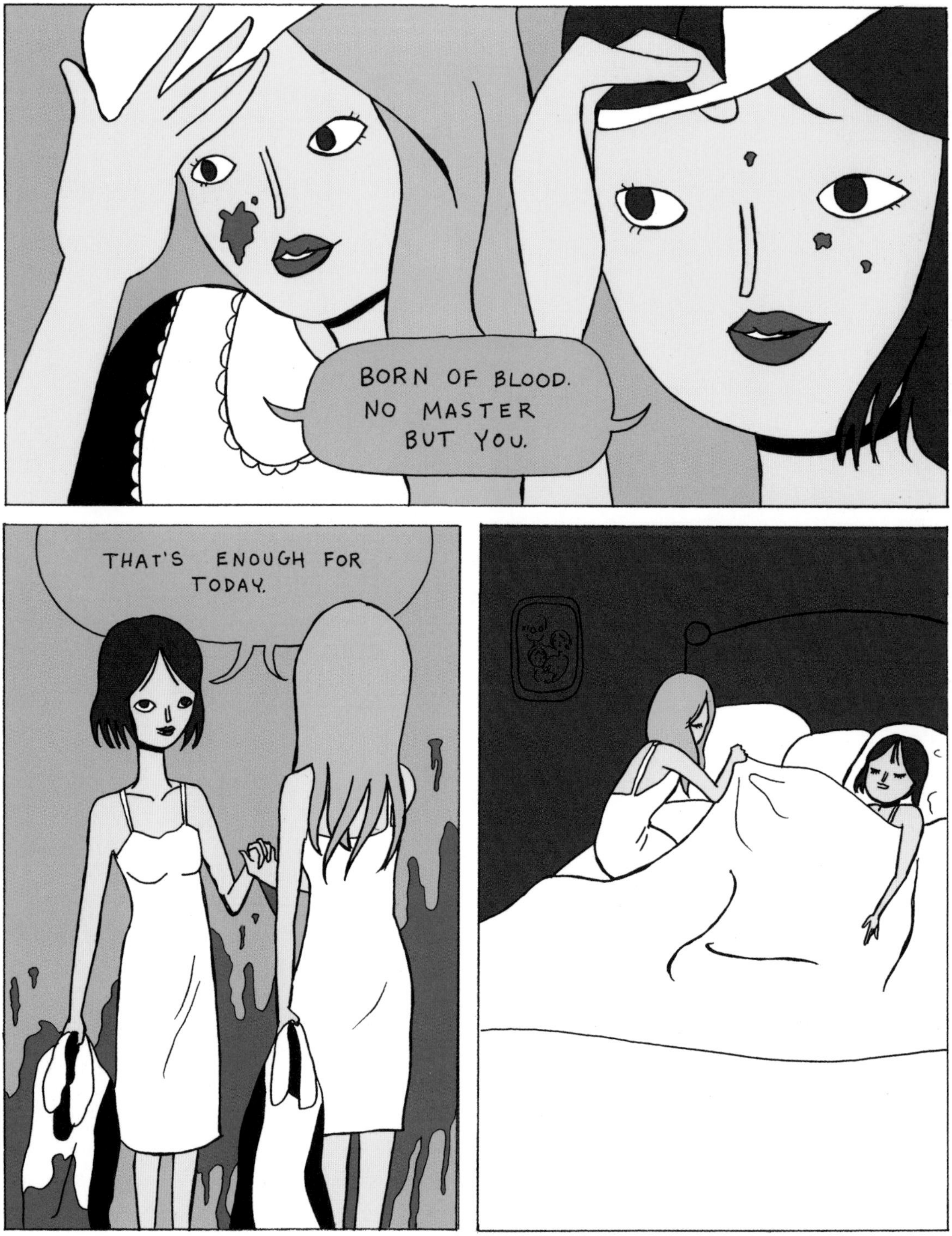
BORN OF BLOOD. NO MASTER BUT YOU.
THAT'S ENOUGH FOR TODAY.

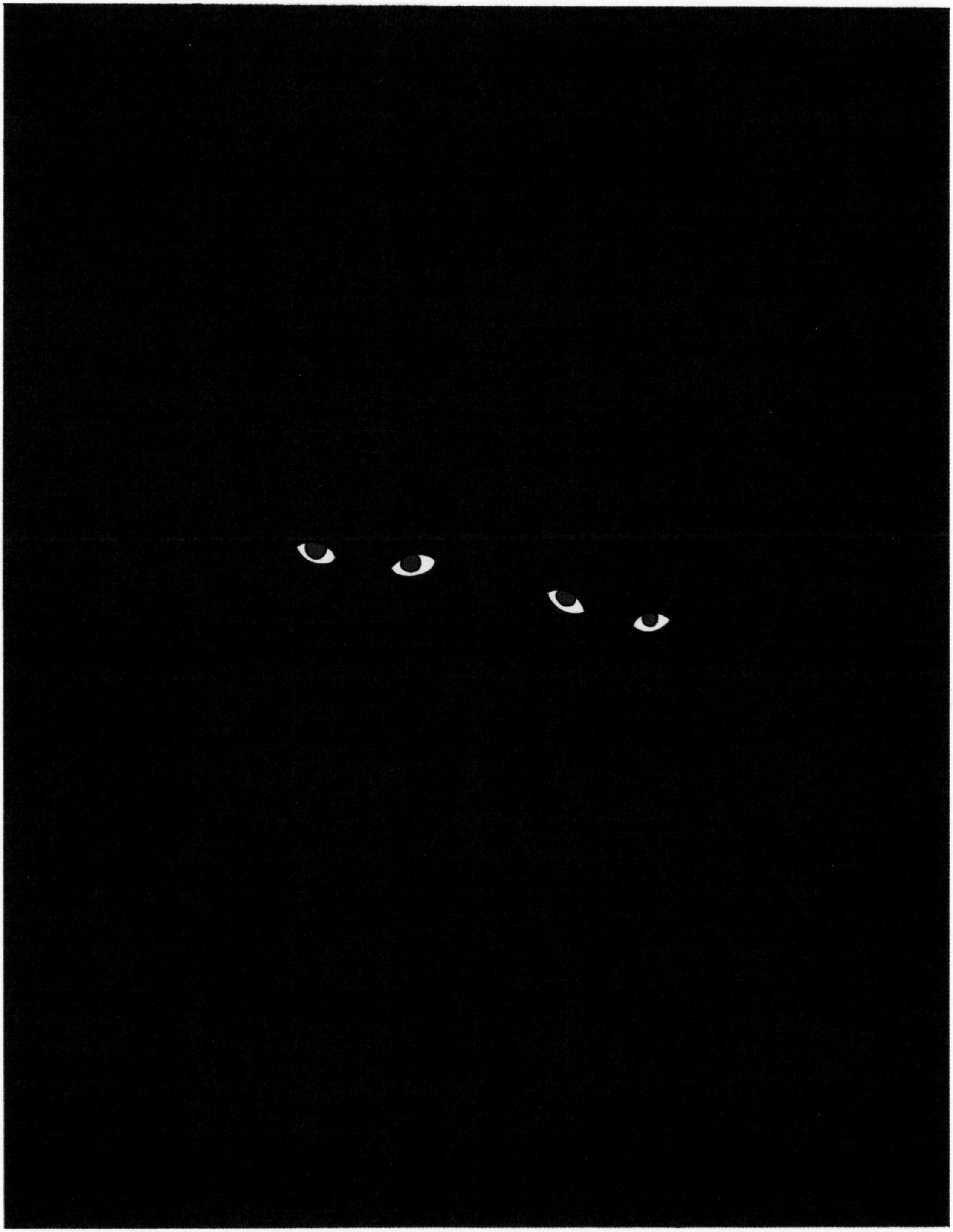

✝

Christine and Lea Papin
were arrested and found guilty of the murders
of Leonie and Genevieve Lancelin.

Christine was sentenced to death by guillotine
and starved herself to death in prison.

Lea was released from prison
after serving eight years. She worked as
a hotel maid until her death in 2001.

Katie Skelly lives and works in New York City. Her previous comics include *My Pretty Vampire*, *The Agency*, *Operation Margarine*, and *Nurse Nurse*. Skelly holds a B.A. in Art History from Syracuse University and was awarded the Emerging Artist Prize at Cartoon Crossroads Columbus in 2015.

She wishes to extend special thanks to Jaime Hernandez, Joe McCulloch, Jennifer Simmons, and Cartoonist Kayfabe.